The Posh
Pescatarian

Stephanie Harris-Uyidi
My Favorite Sustainable Seafood Recipes.

The Posh Pescatarian: My Favorite Sustainable Seafood Recipes

First Edition

Graphic Design and Illustrations by Jessica Ha

Photography by Katherine Tran, Quaid Cde Baca and Stephanie Harris-Uyidi

Library of Congress Cataloging-in-Publication Data

Harris-Uyidi, Stephanie
The Posh Pescatarian: My Favorite Sustainable Seafood Recipes/Harris-Uyidi, Stephanie – 1st ed.
ISBN 13:978-1468144444

Pescatarian

pes·ca·tar·i·an (*noun*) \ pe-ske-ter-ē-en\: one whose diet includes fish but no meat

Source: Merriam-Webster dictionary

Acknowledgments

Creating this book would have proved impossible were it not for the support of an entire network of people, starting with my family. Mom, Dad, Natalie, Leslie, Kimberli and all of my nieces, nephews, aunts, uncles, cousins and in-laws—thank you for always believing in me and providing a constant surge of encouragement and excitement.

Special thanks to my husband, Alain, who has endured countless kitchen experiments (for better or for worse) and several random trips to the market.

To my all-star creative team, Jessica, Katherine, Quaid and Deirdre, thank you for your patients, ideas and sense of humor. I am lucky to have you.

I would be remiss not to mention my incredible YouTube and Facebook supporters who continue to keep me motivated, challenged and inspired.

Finally, thanks to my Creator, who made all of this possible.

* * * *

This book is dedicated to you all!

Introduction

Welcome to my collection of sustainable seafood recipes! Although this is not an exhaustive list of favorites, I have included the recipes that I adore and those that I think you will come to love.

It goes without saying that I enjoy cooking, especially for family and friends. The process of dreaming up a recipe and following the steps to bring it to life puts my heart and mind in a really good place. Preparing a meal is a creative process that is both rewarding and delicious.

Over the years, my focus has been on preparing sustainable seafood. When I learned that I could be responsible for eating the very last red snapper on earth, I quickly changed the way that I shopped.

Shopping for sustainable seafood simply means that I strive to purchase seafood that has been harvested in an eco-friendly manner using appropriate fishing methods (harpooning, hook and lining, trolling, etc.). The list of seafood considered sustainable can change at any given time. To stay informed, be sure to check with reliable sources. I have included a list in the back of the book.

If you enjoy cooking as much as I, then you will be pleased to know that there are myriad recipes contained within this book that you can really sink your teeth into.

Conversely, if you don't like spending much time in the kitchen, you will find recipes that work for your lifestyle as well. From Brazilian Shrimp and Black Bean Empanadas to simple lemony light tuna, there are recipes for everyone.

My moniker is the Posh Pescatarian, but I enjoy a wide variety of foods. In fact, not all of the recipes within feature seafood in a starring role. I have included some of my best recipes for chunky salsas, sauces and side dishes.

Finally, you don't need any special skills or training to make my recipes—just an appetite for adventure! I encourage you to be fearless in the kitchen and use my recipes as a jumping off point for creating your own special meals. Experiment as you will!

Bon appétit!

Stephanie

Stephanie

On Food Styling

The food found throughout this book was prepared and styled by yours truly. I made the decision to do the work myself because I wanted to present you with photos that would give you an honest view of the recipes that you are about to experiment with.

You will also notice repeating food themes, such as wild salmon, cilantro and mango. This is because these ingredients are some of my favorites and a part of my weekly shopping list. Since the idea of this book is to provide you with recipes that I adore and prepare for my family on a regular basis, you will often find food that I typically have on hand.

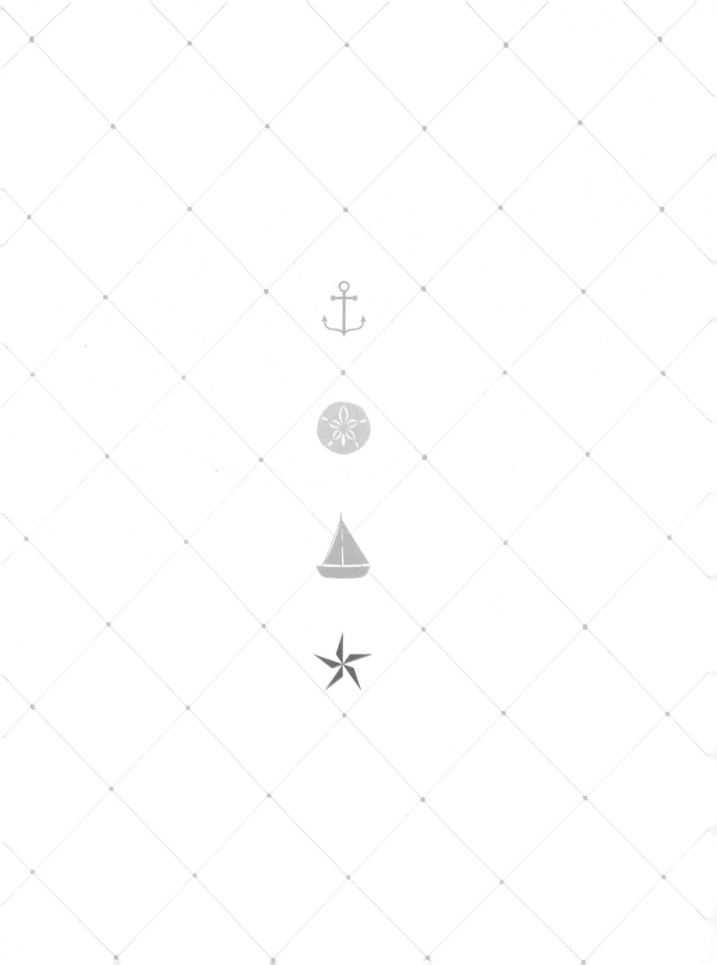

Sustainable Seafood

"Seafood is sustainable when the population of that species of fish is managed in a way that provides for today's needs without damaging the ability of the species to reproduce and be available for future generations."

—*U.S. National Oceanographic and Atmospheric Administration*

Author's Note

Seafood is truly a gift from the sea! In addition to being delicious, seafood is a high-protein, low-fat food that provides a range of health benefits. White-fleshed fish, in particular, is lower in fat than any other source of animal protein, and oily fish are high in omega-3 fatty acids, or the "good" fats. Since the human body can't make significant amounts of these essential nutrients, fish are an important part of the diet. Fish are also low in the "bad" fats (commonly found in red meat) called omega-6 fatty acids.

As much as I enjoy highlighting the benefits of seafood, I would be remiss not to inform you of some of the possible risks. According to expert sources, there are some types of seafood that you should eat infrequently, if at all. Here is the reason—many of our oceans, lakes and rivers are polluted and, as a result, some of the fish that live in these waters are contaminated with mercury, polychlorinated biphenyls (PCB) and other toxins.

The good news is that the risk of mercury poisoning from eating fish and shellfish is not a health concern for most adults, according to the U.S. Food and Drug Administration (FDA). The risks depend on the amount of fish and shellfish eaten and the levels of mercury found within. Pregnant or nursing women and children, however, are the exceptions.

To provide insight on the topic, experts from the Fish 4 Health program (www.fish4health.net) offer consumers free wallet cards and a smartphone app designed to help pregnant or nursing women make informed decisions about the seafood that they consume. The Fish 4 Health program encourages pregnant or nursing women and women that will become pregnant to follow five recommendations that will keep their babies healthy:

1. Consume 8-12 ounces of fish per week.
2. Avoid eating seafood that is high in environmental pollutants, such as mercury or PCBs.
3. Consume fish that provides healthy omega-3 fatty acids (e.g., EPA and DHA).
4. Avoid eating raw fish when pregnant, and avoid serving raw fish to infants or young children.
5. Use caution when eating locally caught seafood (i.e., seafood not purchased in a grocery store or restaurant).

If women follow this advice, program officers are certain that this will reduce their risks from pollutants and increase the health benefits from eating seafood. Funding for the Fish 4 Health program is provided by the National Institute of Health, National Oceanographic and Atmospheric Administration, Environmental Protection Agency and U.S. Department of Agriculture. Expertise is provided by scientists from Purdue University, Indiana Department of Environmental Management, Indiana Department of Health, Rhode Island Sea Grant, Washington Sea Grant, Illinois-Indiana Sea Grant, Texas Sea Grant, Florida Department of Health and the Aquarium of the Pacific (Long Beach). Check out the resources section for more information about healthy and sustainable seafood.

* * * *

The varieties of seafood with the lowest levels of toxins include anchovies, butterfish, clams, cod, Dungeness crab, king crab, snow crab, crawfish, haddock, Atlantic herring, Maine lobster, Atlantic mackerel, blue mussels, oysters, salmon, sardines, bay scallops, shrimp, pink squid and tilapia. Check out the sources section in the back of this book for a detailed list of the best seafood to eat.

Shopping for Seafood

Making the perfect seafood recipe starts with selecting the perfect seafood. The following is a compilation of tips from the U.S. Food and Drug Administration, Environmental Defense Fund and good old common sense.

The process starts by buying seafood from a retailer who follows proper food handling practices. This helps ensure that the seafood you are purchasing is safe and high quality. I encourage you to go the extra mile and check out a market's seafood counter carefully. Does it look and smell clean?

How to Choose Fresh Fish

The key to buying perfect seafood is to only buy fish that is refrigerated or properly iced. Fish should be displayed on a thick bed of fresh ice that is not melting, and preferably in a case or under some type of cover. Other tips:

- Fish should smell fresh and mild, not fishy, sour or ammonia-like.
- A fish's eyes should be clear and bulge a little (except for a few naturally cloudy-eyed fish types, such as walleye pike).
- Whole fish and filets should have firm, shiny flesh and bright red gills free from slime. Dull flesh could mean the fish is old. Note: Fish fillets that have been previously frozen may have lost some of their shine, but they are fine to eat.
- The flesh should spring back when pressed.
- Fish fillets should display no darkening or drying around the edges. They should have no green or yellowish discoloration, and should not appear dry or mushy in any areas.

It is important to look for freshness when choosing seafood. In some species, if the catch has been left out in the sun too long—or the fish haven't been transported under proper refrigeration—toxins known as scombrotoxins, or histamines, can develop. Eating spoiled fish that have high levels of these toxins can cause illness.

Today, fresh catches can be processed and frozen immediately to very low temperatures—frequently, this takes place right on the fishing vessel. However, frozen seafood can spoil if the fish thaws during transport and is left at warm temperatures for too long. To help ensure that the frozen fish you're buying is safe, follow these guidelines:

- Don't buy frozen seafood if its package is open, torn or crushed on the edges.
- Avoid packages that are positioned above the "frost line" or top of the freezer case in the store's freezer.
- If the package cover is transparent, look for signs of frost or ice crystals. These could mean the fish has been stored a long time or thawed and refrozen—in which case, choose another package.

Put seafood on ice or in the refrigerator or freezer soon after buying it, using these guidelines for safe storage:

- If seafood will be used within two days after purchase, store it in the refrigerator.
- If seafood won't be used within two days after purchase, wrap it tightly in moisture-proof freezer paper or foil to protect it from air leaks, and store it in the freezer.

Thaw It Safely

Thaw frozen seafood gradually by placing it in the refrigerator overnight. If you have to thaw seafood quickly, either seal it in a plastic bag and immerse it in cold water, or—if the food will be cooked immediately thereafter—microwave it on the defrost setting and stop the defrost cycle while the fish is still icy but pliable.

Cook It Properly

Most seafood should be cooked to an internal temperature of 145°F. But if you don't have a food thermometer, there are other ways to determine whether seafood is done.

- Fish: Slip the point of a sharp knife into the flesh and pull it aside. The flesh should be opaque and separate easily. If you cooked the fish in the microwave, check it in more than one spot to help ensure doneness.
- Shrimp and Lobster: The flesh becomes pearly-opaque.
- Scallops: The flesh turns milky white or opaque and firm.
- Clams, Mussels and Oysters: Watch for the point at which their shells open, which means they're done. Throw out the ones that don't open.

Temperature Counts

Follow these serving guidelines once your seafood is cooked and ready to be enjoyed.

- Never leave seafood or other perishable food out of the refrigerator for more than 2 hours—or, for more than 1 hour when temperatures are above 90°F. Bacteria that can cause illness grow quickly at warm temperatures (temperatures between 40°F and 140°F).
- Carry picnic seafood in a cooler with a cold pack or ice. When possible, put the cooler in the shade. Keep the lid closed as much of the time as you can.
- When it's party time, keep hot seafood hot and cold seafood cold: Divide hot party dishes containing seafood into smaller serving platters. Keep platters refrigerated until time to reheat them for serving. Keep cold seafood on ice or serve it throughout the gathering from platters kept in the refrigerator.

Pregnant women, older adults, and people with weakened immune systems have an increased chance of getting a foodborne illness called listeriosis. If you are in one of these groups, there is a simple step you can take to reduce your chance of contracting the listeriosis disease from seafood: Avoid refrigerated types of smoked seafood except in a cooked recipe, such as a casserole.

Refrigerated smoked seafood, such as salmon, trout, whitefish, cod, tuna or mackerel, is usually labeled as "nova-style," "lox," "kippered," "smoked," or "jerky" and can be found in the refrigerated section of grocery stores and delicatessens. They should be avoided. You needn't worry about getting listeriosis from canned or shelf-stable smoked seafood.

It's always best to cook seafood thoroughly to minimize the risk of foodborne illness. However, if you choose to eat raw fish anyway, one rule of thumb is to eat fish that has been previously frozen.

- Some species of fish can contain parasites, and freezing will kill any parasites that may be present.
- However, be aware that freezing doesn't kill all harmful microorganisms. That's why the safest route is to cook your seafood.

Legend has it that oysters are safe to eat only in months ending with the letter "R." This rumor came about at a time when refrigeration controls that we have today were nonexistent. These days, shellfish are strictly regulated through a federal-state-industry cooperative program which helps make them safe to eat year round. The program is known as the National Shellfish Sanitation Program (NSSP).

Through the cooperative program, the Food and Drug Administration (FDA), state regulatory agencies, and the shellfish industry work together to keep molluscan shellfish (such as oysters, clams, and mussels) safe for consumption by adhering to strict controls on their growing, harvesting, processing, packaging and transport.

Follow the guidelines below from the U.S. Food and Drug Administration (USFDA) to ensure ultimate shellfish safety.

Selecting Shellfish: Some Special Guidelines

The USFDA requires shellfish harvesters and processors of oysters, clams and mussels to put a tag on sacks or containers of live shellfish (in the shell), and a label on containers or packages of shucked shellfish. These tags and labels contain specific information about the product, including a certification number for the processor, which means that the shellfish were harvested and processed in accordance with national shellfish safety controls. Ask to see the tag or check the label when purchasing shellfish.

Selecting Shellfish: Some Special Guidelines

1. **Discard Cracked/Broken Ones**: Throw away clams, oysters and mussels if their shells are cracked or broken.
2. **Do a "Tap Test"**: Live clams, oysters and mussels will close up when the shell is tapped. If they don't close when tapped, do not select them.
3. **Check for Leg Movement**: Live crabs and lobsters should show some leg movement. They spoil rapidly after death, so only live crabs and lobsters should be selected and prepared.

Catching your own fish can be an exhilarating experience, but there are a few safety tips you should keep in mind.

Before venturing out, always check local advisories and sign postings for information about the safety of fish and shellfish in your area.

During your fishing adventure, be sure to keep fish and shellfish well iced while fishing and while transporting the seafood home.

After your trip, be mindful that some fish caught in some lakes and streams may have harmful levels of polychlorinated biphenyls, or PCBs, which can cause a variety of health problems. Since PCBs accumulate in fat, trim the fat and skin from fish before cooking. This can lessen the risk of exposure to these contaminants. Broil, grill or bake the trimmed, skinned fish on a rack so the fat drips away.

Note that harmful levels of PCBs have not been found in fish that are sold in the commercial marketplace, including farm-raised species.

Table of Contents

Appetizers

Main Dishes

Soups & Chowders

Sides & Extras

Sauces & Spice Blends

Appetizers

Appetizers, hors d'oeuvres, starters — whatever you call them, these delicious pre-meal delicacies can help set the stage for your main meal. Depending on the size of the crowd and my budget, I typically serve two to three appetizers for an event. Consider hosting a cocktail party and serving five to six appetizers as the main course.

Caribbean Salt Cod Fritters

Inspired by the variations of this snack found throughout the Caribbean, these salt cod fritters are the perfect beginning to any meal. Keep in mind that you will have to prepare the salt cod one day in advance for best results.

Ingredients

· Serves 6-8 ·

½ pound Pacific salt cod

3 cups cold water

1 cup all-purpose flour, sifted

1 egg, lightly beaten

6 ounces milk

1 medium onion, finely chopped

¼ cup green onion (tops only), chopped

1 small habañero or Scotch bonnet pepper, seeded and finely chopped

1 teaspoon baking powder

1 teaspoon cayenne pepper

1 teaspoon ground thyme

1 tablespoon all spice

1 teaspoon granulated garlic

½ teaspoon sea salt, reserve some for garnish

Vegetable oil for deep frying. Use canola, sunflower or another oil with a high smoke point.

Directions

Prepare the fish

Soak the salt cod in water overnight, changing out the water every 4 to 6 hours to remove the salt. Drain and rinse the fish well. Remove any bones or skin. Place the fish in a saucepan and cover with 3 cups of cold water. Bring the fish to a boil and reduce the heat to medium. Cover the pan and simmer for 10 minutes. After 10 minutes, drain the fish and rinse it under cold water.

When cool enough to handle, flake the fish and set it aside. Now would be a good time to heat your oven to 200°F and to start heating your frying oil to 375°F.

Prepare the batter

Mix the flour, baking powder, cayenne pepper, ground thyme, all spice, granulated garlic and sea salt together in a large bowl. Make a well in the center of the bowl and pour in the egg and milk. Mix together to make a batter. Next, gently fold in the onion, habañero pepper and flaked fish. Keep in mind that the moisture level in flour varies depending on the humidity in your kitchen, so you may need to add more flour or milk as needed to make the ideal fritter batter.

Fry the fritters

Drop tablespoons of the mixture into the hot oil. Use a wooden spoon or a chopstick to keep them from sticking together. Fry the fritters for 3-4 minutes, turning once or twice until golden brown. Remove the fritters from the oil using a slotted spoon. Drain the fritters on paper towels or a cooling rack. Keep them warm by placing completed batches in the oven while frying the remaining fritters. Serve immediately with your choice of dipping sauce.

Halibut Ceviche with Mango and Habañero

Ceviche is essentially raw fish marinated in citric acid, such as lemon, lime or grapefruit juice. The acid in the juice helps "cook" the fish by changing its texture.

My first experience with ceviche was on the island of St. Barths while on my honeymoon. I don't remember the restaurant, but I do remember that the day was warm and the ceviche was cool, and delicious. Hubby and I shared a second serving. It was the perfect day!

When I got home, I began experimenting with different ingredients and flavor combinations to create my own recipe. I discovered that the beauty of a good ceviche lies in the balance between using very fresh fish and enhancing it with simple ingredients. I think mine hits the mark.

Ingredients

• Serves 2-3 •

½ pound Pacific halibut, boneless and skinless, diced

6 large limes

Zest of 2 limes

1 tablespoon freshly grated ginger

2 medium mangoes, seeded, peeled and diced

½ cup red onion, diced

1 teaspoon fresh habañero pepper, minced

1 tablespoon olive oil

Sea salt to taste

White pepper to taste

Directions

Rinse the fish and pat it dry. In a bowl large enough to fit the entire fillet, add the fish, zest from 1 lime, juice from 4 of limes and ginger. Cover the bowl with plastic wrap and place in the refrigerator for 4 hours.

When the fish is ready, drain the liquid and chop the fish into small bite-sized chunks. Add the juice of 1 lime and marinate for an additional 30 minutes. When the time is up, drain the bowl and add the habañero pepper, red onion, olive oil, mango, salt and pepper, and the juice of the remaining lime. Mix and serve immediately.

Gulf Coast Crawfish Cornbread

Also known as crawdads, crayfish or mudbugs, crawfish from the Gulf Coast of the United States are not only sustainable—they are also the best tasting! You can serve this crawfish cornbread as an appetizer or offer it alongside a healthy serving of red beans and rice.

Ingredients

· Serves 10-12 ·

1 small Spanish onion, chopped finely

1 cup bell pepper, chopped finely

½ cup green onion (green part only), chopped finely

Vegetable oil for sautéing

2 tablespoons of diced green chili, medium heat

½ teaspoon white pepper

½ cup white flour, sifted

1½ cups corn meal

4 teaspoons baking powder

½ teaspoon baking soda

1 teaspoon sea salt

½ cup vegetable oil

3 large eggs

1 cup skim milk

1½ cups of blended shredded cheese; I recommend cheddar, Monterey jack and parmesan

1 pound U.S. cooked crawfish tails

1 teaspoon herbes de Provence

Directions

Sauté the Spanish onions, green onion and bell pepper in a small amount of vegetable oil until the onions are transparent. Add the diced green chili and white pepper and cook for 1 minute. Set aside to cool. In a large bowl, mix together the flour, corn meal, baking powder, baking soda, sea salt, vegetable oil, eggs and milk. Next fold in the onion mixture, shredded cheese, herbes de Provençe and the crawfish. Pour into a lightly greased 13x9-inch pan and bake in a 400°F oven for 35 minutes, or pour into muffin tins and bake for 25 minutes.

Olive Tapenade with Anchovy

I love this olive paste, or tapenade, on baguette slices, as a sandwich spread, atop fish or served with crudités. I used my mortar and pestle to make this rustic version, but you can use your food processor if so inclined.

Ingredients

• Makes ½ cup •

½ cup of your favorite blend of black and green French olives, pitted

6 flat anchovy filets

1 large garlic clove

2 tablespoon capers, rinsed and drained

1 tablespoon fresh lemon juice

1 teaspoon fresh thyme

¼ cup extra virgin olive oil

Directions

Add the olives and capers to your mortar and pound to a chunky consistency. Place in a medium-sized bowl. Add the anchovies to the mortar along with the thyme and garlic clove and pound to a paste. Add to the bowl with the olives. Add the olive oil and lemon juice to the bowl and mix to combine. Taste and correct the seasoning as needed. Cover and refrigerate for 15 minutes prior to serving.

Fried Calamari Strips

Although not a huge fan of seafood, my mother, Betty, is the ultimate connoisseur of fried calamari. I'm not sure what it is, but there is something about deep-fried squid that makes her smile. So, as one would imagine, I was tickled pink when she gave my recipe the thumbs up.

Ingredients

· Serves 5-6 ·

3 pounds calamari steaks, cut into finger-width strips

Sea salt and fresh cracked black pepper to taste

2 tablespoons dried parsley

¼ cup olive oil

3-4 cups all-purpose flour

Oil for deep frying

Lemon wedges for serving

Directions

In a large bowl, toss the calamari strips with the salt, pepper, parsley and olive oil until well coated.

Cover the bowl with plastic wrap or a lid and place it in the refrigerator overnight. When ready to cook, drain the calamari to remove any residual liquid. Place the flour in a large bowl. Add the calamari one handful at a time and toss to coat. Do this in small batches until you have coated all of the calamari. Once coated, allow the calamari to rest for 5 minutes before frying—this will help the flour to form a crust.

While the calamari is resting, heat your frying oil to 375°F. Fry the calamari in small batches until light golden brown. Drain on paper towels and serve with lemon wedges or a sauce of your choice.

Mini Crab Corn Muffins

This is one of the best ways to turn one pound of crab meat into 48 servings—the trick is to use a mini muffin tin. Definitely one of hubby's favorites!

Ingredients

• Makes 48 mini muffins •

1 pound Dungeness crab meat (picked over to remove any shells)

3 large eggs

1½ cups white cheddar cheese, shredded

1 cup chopped bell pepper, chopped finely

½ cup green onion, chopped (green part only)

1 small Spanish onion, chopped finely

2 tablespoons pimiento pepper, chopped

½ cup roasted frozen corn

1½ cups corn meal

½ cup all-purpose flour

½ teaspoon white pepper

4 teaspoons baking powder

½ teaspoon baking soda

1 teaspoon sea salt

½ cup vegetable oil

1 cup skim milk

Directions

Sauté the Spanish onion, green onion and bell pepper in a small amount of vegetable oil until the Spanish onions become transparent. Add the pimiento pepper, frozen roasted corn and white pepper, and cook for 1 minute. Set aside to cool. In a large bowl, mix together the flour, corn meal, baking powder, baking soda, sea salt, eggs, vegetable oil and milk. Next gently fold in the cooked onion mixture, shredded cheese and the crab. Pour into lightly greased muffin tins and bake at 375°F for 20 minutes. Let cool on a rack for 5 minutes before serving.

Thai Salmon Cakes

Chances are that when visiting my home, you will be served two things—a yummy libation (or two) and my flavorful Thai salmon cakes. These tasty bites are as easy to make as they are delicious. This recipe calls for the use of prepared Thai sweet chili sauce, which is available in most markets.

Ingredients

• Serves 10-12 •

¼ cup fresh cilantro (leaves and stems), chopped

¼ cup red onion, chopped

3 (6-ounce) cans of boneless, skinless salmon, drained

¼ cup panko bread crumbs

Sea salt and pepper to taste

¼ cup Thai sweet chili sauce, plus additional sauce for serving

Zest and juice of 1 small lemon

2 eggs

Oil for frying

Lime wedges for serving

Directions

In a food processor blend together the cilantro, red onion and salmon until just combined. Place the mixture in a large bowl and add the panko bread crumbs, salt, pepper, Thai sweet chili sauce, lemon zest, lemon juice and eggs. Mix well. Place the mixture in the refrigerator to chill for 30 minutes. Once the mixture has chilled, use a spoon to make 1-ounce patties. Place the finished patties on a baking sheet and put them back in the refrigerator to chill for 10 minutes. While the patties are chilling, heat the oil in a shallow skillet to 350°F. Remove the patties from the refrigerator and fry them until golden brown. Serve with Thai sweet chili sauce and a side of lime wedges.

Seaweed Steamers

The combination of succulent clams and earthy kelp
makes this recipe an ideal treat any day of the year.

Ingredients

· Serves 4-5 ·

¾ pound live hard-shell clams (littlenecks, cherry stone or steamer clams)

1 gallon of water

⅓ cup coarse kosher salt

½ cup Spanish onion, finely diced

1 garlic clove, chopped

2 tablespoons unsalted butter

1 ounce dried kelp (seaweed), cut into small pieces

Zest of 1 lemon

2 tablespoons sea salt

3 cups water

1 cup white wine

2 tablespoons olive oil

¼ cup chopped parsley

Your favorite bread for dipping

Prepare clams

Prepare the clams by soaking them in the kosher salt and gallon water for 1 hour. This will help to remove the sand from the clams. Be sure to use kosher or sea salt, as the iodine in regular salt will kill the clams before they hit the boiling water.

In a pot large enough to hold all of the clams, sauté the garlic and onion in olive oil and butter until softened. Add the kelp, lemon zest, sea salt, water and wine and simmer for 10 minutes. Add the clams and ½ the parsley. Close the pot with a tight-fitting lid. Cook the clams until they have opened—about 10 minutes. Serve the clams in bowls topped with a sprinkle of parsley and a piece of bread for dipping.

Plantain-Wrapped Rock Shrimp with Guava Yogurt

The sweetness of ripe plantains combined with the delicate, succulent flavor of Florida rock shrimp is a delicious combination, while the tartness of the guava yogurt helps balance the flavors. Rest assured that your hard work in slicing the plantains will be rewarded!

Ingredients

• Serves 4-5 •

2 tablespoons guava paste

½ cup store-bought strained Greek yogurt

½ pound Florida rock shrimp, peeled and deveined

4 ripe plantains

1 teaspoon orange zest

Sea salt

1 teaspoon ancho chili powder

1 tablespoon olive oil

Oil for frying

20-30 toothpicks, soaked in water

For the guava yogurt

Add the guava paste to a microwavable bowl and microwave on high for 20 seconds—this will make it more malleable. Add the yogurt to the bowl and mix well. Wrap the bowl with cling film and place it in the refrigerator until ready to use.

For the shrimp and plantains

Start by seasoning the shrimp with the sea salt, ancho chili powder, orange zest and olive oil. Mix to blend the flavors. Cover and allow them to marinate in the refrigerator until the plantains are prepared.

Peel the plantains and slice them lengthwise as thin as possible without comprising their strength. Use a mandoline to get the slices as even as possible. If you don't own a mandolin, use a vegetable peeler or cheese slicer can do the trick. Add the slices to a baking sheet until all of the plantains have been sliced. Continue until all of the plantains have been sliced. When done, you should have 15-20 slices.

Next take 1 slice of plantain and 1 shrimp and wrap the plantain around the shrimp. Use a toothpick to hold it together. If the plantain slices are not malleable enough and break when wrapping the shrimp, place them in a to 250°F oven for 10 minutes to soften.

Continue until all of the shrimp have been wrapped. To cook the shrimp, heat about ½ cup of vegetable oil on medium in a large frying pan. Add the shrimp. Cook for 3 minutes on each side until brown. Drain on paper towels. Serve with the guava yogurt.

Smoked Oyster Crostini

This decadent appetizer is the apex of affordable luxury. You can use tinned smoked oysters bathed in olive oil, or you can purchase freshly smoked oysters. If you choose the latter, you will need to add about ⅓ cup of olive oil to this recipe.

Ingredients

• Makes 2 dozen crostini •

2 dozen smoked oysters in olive oil, drained (reserve oil)

1 baguette, sliced into 24 rounds

3 or 4 garlic cloves

Chopped chives for garnish

Directions

Place the baguette slices on a baking sheet and brush them with the reserved oyster olive oil. Place the pan under the broiler until bread is toasted light golden brown, about 2 minutes. Remove the baguette slices from the broiler. Cut the tip off of a garlic clove and rub each slice of bread with it. Place one oyster on each baguette slice. Garnish with chopped chives and serve.

Smoked Trout Spread

My sister, Leslie, is a huge fan of this recipe. Inspired by the delicious flavor of smoked trout in olive oil, I wanted to create a multipurpose recipe that could be used as a dip for crudités or as a spread for crackers, bagels or tea sandwiches.

Ingredients

• Makes 1½ cups •

6 ounces cream cheese, softened

1 teaspoon lemon zest

2 tablespoon fresh chives, chopped

6 ounces smoked trout in olive oil, drained and flaked (reserve oil for other use*)

Juice of ½ a lemon

Sea salt to taste

Directions

By hand or with a mixer, blend the cream cheese with the lemon zest, lemon juice and chives. Gently fold in the smoked trout. Taste the spread and add sea salt as desired. Allow the mix to chill in the refrigerator for 15 minutes prior to serving.

*Add olive oil to the reserved trout oil and serve as dipping sauce for bread, or combine with lemon juice for a salad dressing.

Grilled Shrimp & Pineapple Cocktail

One of my favorite ways to prepare pineapple is on the grill. The heat from the grill brings out its sweetness. I created this recipe a few years ago when I found myself with a few pieces of grilled pineapple and a handful of shrimp left over from a party. I combined the two with a few other simple ingredients and created a signature dish. This recipe also works well will grilled sea scallops.

Ingredients

· Serves 2 ·

1 pound U.S. shrimp, peeled and deveined

Sea salt and white pepper to taste

3 tablespoons olive oil

1 medium-sized pineapple, pared, cored and cut into round slices

¼ cup cilantro, chopped

¼ cup red onion, chopped

1 tomato, chopped

1 large lime, zest and juice

· Optional ·

Fancy serving glasses

Directions

Start by turning the grill pan to medium high. While it's heating up, season the shrimp with salt, white pepper and 1 tablespoon of olive oil, and set aside.

When the grill is hot, add the pineapple slices. Grill on each side for about 2 to 3 minutes—be sure to get nice grill marks on the fruit for presentation purposes. When done, set the pineapple aside and allow them to cool. When cool, chop into bite-sized pieces.

Next grill the shrimp until done—about 2 minutes on both sides. Be sure not to overcook. Set the shrimp aside and allow them to cool. When cool, chop each shrimp in half widthwise.

To assemble the cocktail, add the pineapple and shrimp to a medium-sized bowl. Add the remaining 2 tablespoons of olive oil, lime juice, lime zest, cilantro, tomato, and red onion, season with salt and pepper to taste, and mix. Place in glasses and serve.

Open-Faced Sardine Sandwich

Hands down one of my favorite ways to enjoy tinned sardines, this sandwich is a delicious everyday treat that also goes over well at posh cocktail parties. I love to use pickled lemon and English cucumber to add texture and signature flavor.

An added benefit of this recipe is the nutritional value—sardines have been singled out as a "super food." Three ounces of the fish contain more calcium than a glass of milk, and they are loaded with omega-3 fatty acid, packed with protein and are highly sustainable.

Ingredients

• Serves 10 •

2 (4 ounce) tins of boneless, skinless sardines in olive oil (separate the oil from the fish)

2 tablespoons capers

¼ cup red onion, chopped

1 teaspoon crushed red pepper flakes

1 French baguette, sliced into 10 rounds

1 tomato, diced

1 English cucumber, sliced into 20 rounds

2 pickled lemons, sliced into 20 rounds

1 garlic clove, peeled

2 tablespoons fresh cracked peppercorns

Directions

Make the filling by crumbling the sardines into a medium-sized bowl. Add the capers, crushed red pepper flakes, red onion and tomato. Mix well. Refrigerate for 10 minutes.

Turn on the oven broiler.

Place the French baguette slices on a cookie sheet and slightly brush 1 side with the reserved sardine oil. Next, cut the tip off of the garlic clove and rub it on each slice of bread. When done, place the toast in the broiler for 2 minutes or until light golden brown. Remove from the broiler and set aside.

Assemble the sandwiches by layering each slice of baguette with 2 English cucumber slices and 2 slices of pickled lemon. Top with the sardine filling and garnish with the fresh cracked peppercorns. Serve immediately.

Salmon Jerky

My salmon jerky is a family delicacy and a particular favorite of my husband, Alain, and my brother-in-law, Leonard. I make this recipe at least twice a year and experiment with new ingredients. This particular recipe is one of my favorites because it enhances the natural flavor of the salmon and adds a bit of sweetness.

The three most important tools that you will need for this recipe are a good fresh fish, a food dehydrator and a lot of patience—the drying process takes roughly 8–10 hours. It's worth it!

Ingredients

· Serves 6-8 ·

2 cups water

2 cups soy sauce

3 pounds skin-on fresh salmon fillet

2 cups dark brown sugar

2 tablespoons honey

1 bay leaf

3 tablespoons fresh ginger, grated

2 limes, zest and juice

· Optional crusting ingredients ·

Freshly cracked peppercorns

Coarse sea salt

Granulated orange peel

Black sesame seeds

· Special equipment ·

Food dehydrator

Directions

In a sauce pan, add the water, soy sauce, brown sugar, honey, ginger, bay leaf and lime zest. On medium heat, cook until the sugar and honey dissolve. Set aside and allow the sauce to cool completely.

Pick over the salmon and remove any bones—use kitchen tweezers or clean needle-nose pliers. You have two options at this point to make either jerky strips or jerky bites, or both.

For strips, use a sharp knife or kitchen shears and slice the fish lengthwise. Keep in mind that the thicker the slice, the longer the drying time. For the jerky bites, cut the fish into 1½-inch cubes. When finished, add the fish to a large bowl along with the marinade. Refrigerate for 24 hours.

When ready, gently drain the bowl and add the fish to a bed of paper towels, blotting off excess marinade. The wetter the fish, the longer the drying time.

If you are crusting the fish with freshly cracked peppercorns, coarse sea salt, granulated orange peel or black sesame seeds, now is the time to do so.

To dry the salmon, place the fish on the drying racks of a food dehydrator (per the equipment instructions) and allow it to dry for 2 hours. After 2 hours, turn the fish and continue drying for 6 hours. After 6 hours, taste the fish for your ideal level of dryness. If the fish is too moist continue drying for another 2 hours. The jerky should be translucent when properly dried.

When done, remove the fish from the dehydrator and enjoy. Store remaining jerky it in an airtight container in the refrigerator.

Main Dishes

This section includes some of my favorite go-to recipes for weekday meals and special occasions. These recipes go beyond supper and can be used for lunch, brunch and in some cases appetizers (just reduce the portion sizes). In certain cases, you can substitute the species of fish that I recommend for something that you have on hand or for the type of seafood that you find available locally. Once you have tried each dish my way, I encourage you to color outside the lines and use my recipes as a guide to help create your own unique meals.

Brazilian Black Bean & Shrimp Empanadas

Empanadas are the national dish of Brazil. I had the fortune of visiting this beautiful and diverse country several years ago, and flavors of the region stay with me. This empanada is different from the hand-held version that you may be familiar with. The Brazilian version is a bit heartier and served like a deep-dish pie.

Ingredients

· Makes about 6–8 single serving pies (3–4 inches) ·

· For the crust ·

2 cups all-purpose flour

5½ ounces cold butter, cut into pieces

2 eggs, divided (1 whole egg plus 1 yolk for crust, and 1 white for egg wash)

½ teaspoon baking powder

½ teaspoon sea salt

Cold water, as needed

· For the filling ·

12 ounces cooked shrimp

⅓ cup cooked black beans

⅓ cup finely chopped green olives

⅓ cup finely chopped hearts of palm or artichoke hearts (fresh or in water, not marinated)

½ onion, finely chopped

2 tablespoons all-purpose flour

2 tablespoons tomato paste

About ½ cup–1 cup vegetable broth

Sea salt to taste

· Special tools ·

Mini pie pans or small ramekins

Directions

The crust

The easiest way to make the crust is with a food processor. If you don't have a food processor, this can be done by hand using a fork. Combine the dry ingredients with the butter and pulse until the butter is cut into the flour. Add 1 whole egg and the yolk of the other and pulse until they are incorporated. Pulse while adding enough cold water to just bring the dough together. Transfer to a clean surface and bring the dough together into a clump. If it's too sticky, add a little more flour. If it's too dry, add a little more liquid but do not knead the dough.

The filling

In a skillet, sauté the onions until soft. Add the olives, hearts of palm or artichokes, black beans, shrimp and tomato paste. Mix well. Sprinkle the flour on top and stir to incorporate it. Add the broth slowly in increments. Mix well after each addition. Use just enough liquid to get a pasty filling. Heat through and season with salt. Now it's ready to use.

Assemble pies

To assemble the pies, roll out the dough to fit into the mini pie pans or ramekins so there is a little overhang. You'll also need a top crust. The dough is not very sticky, but you may need to lightly sprinkle flour on it every few passes. Roll out the dough as thin as you want (thick crust or thin crust) and lay it in the mold. Add the filling. For best results, use enough of the mix to fill a little over the level of the mold, be sure to press down gently to compact the filling. Place the top crust on and pinch the top and bottom doughs together. To keep the pies from popping open, roll the seam inward. Be sure to pinch and roll the seam shut. If you just pinch the seam, the empanada will come open during baking. Brush lightly with egg white and bake in 375°F oven until golden, about 25-30 minutes. Serve warm or at room temperature.

Curaçao Cod (Bakiou)

If you are looking for a dish to replace your standard baked fish recipe, this is it. Filled with bright flavors, this cod, or bakiou, recipe is influenced by the flavors of the island of Curaçao. I adapted this recipe from one that I found on the Curaçao tourist board website that calls for salted cod. I make it at least three times a month. The recipe works well with rock fish, tilapia, swai and most white-fleshed fish.

Ingredients

• Serves 4-6 •

2 pounds boneless cod, cut into bite-sized pieces

1 cup all-purpose flour

2 tablespoons olive oil

2 tablespoons ghee (traditional Indian clarified butter used for cooking)

1 large onion, sliced

2 tablespoons water

2 cloves garlic, minced

1 red bell pepper, seeded and cut lengthwise julienne style

1 green bell pepper, seeded and cut lengthwise julienne style

3 large tomatoes, peeled and coarsely chopped

1 tablespoon cumin powder

¼ cup minced parsley

Sea salt and freshly cracked black pepper to taste

2 cups cooked rice

Directions

Start by pan frying the fish. Add the olive oil to a medium-heat skillet. Dust each piece of cod with flour and add to the pan. Brown each piece of fish, but do not cook through completely. Remove the fish from the pan and set aside.

Next add ghee to the pan along with the chopped onions, garlic, red pepper, green pepper, tomato, cumin, parsley and black pepper. Sauté for 10 minutes. Add the water, stir and cover the pan. Cook for another 5 minutes. Serve with cooked rice.

Cilantro Lime Rock Shrimp Tacos

The flavors of cilantro and lime are wonderful together. Combining them with succulent Florida rock shrimp and the pleasant texture of corn tortillas makes my taco recipe ideal for groups or parties. The marinade also serves as a sauce, enveloping the shrimp in flavor. You can substitute white fish, such as tilapia, swai or cod, with equally fabulous results.

Ingredients

· Serves 5-6 ·

1 pound Florida rock shrimp

2 large limes, zest and juice

White pepper

1 cup cilantro, leaves and stems

2 garlic cloves

1 cup plus 1 tablespoon olive oil (divided use)

1 tablespoon water

Sea salt

6 corn tortillas

1 cup red cabbage, shredded finely

Directions

Start by seasoning the shrimp with the zest of both limes and white pepper. Make the cilantro lime marinade by adding the cilantro, garlic and the lime juice to a blender. Turn the blender to medium and slowly drizzle in 1 cup olive oil. The marinade will begin to come together. Add the tablespoon of water if the mix is too thick. Add marinade to the shrimp and refrigerate for 15 minutes.

Cook the shrimp by adding the remaining tablespoon of olive oil to a skillet on medium-high heat, then adding the shrimp and marinade. Cook for 6 minutes, until the shrimp are tender and cooked through. Set aside and prepare the tortillas. My preferred method is to heat them over the open flame of a gas range—for a safer method, add a little oil to a skillet and warm them on both sides. Serve the tacos by adding the shrimp to the corn tortillas and topping them with the red cabbage.

Fish en Papillote

I love my fish en papillote, or fish in parchment paper, recipe because it offers a beautiful and stylish way of presenting a meal. Wrapping the fish in parchment paper allows the fish to gently steam in its own juices, keeping it moist and succulent.

I enjoy making this at home in the oven, but my favorite use for this recipe is in the great outdoors. I simply exchange the parchment paper for tin foil and place each packet on the grill or barbeque. For an adventurous touch, try wrapping the fish in banana leaf, followed by a layer of foil.

Ingredients

· Serves 2 ·

2 (6-ounce) pieces of fish; my favorites are wild salmon,
black cod, halibut and Gulf shrimp, or one small whole fish
1 lemon, sliced in 6 rounds
2 tablespoons capers
1 tablespoons fresh tarragon, minced
1 large tomato, diced
Sea salt and white pepper to taste
If using white fish, add 1 teaspoon of olive oil or butter to each packet

Directions

Preheat oven to 400°F.

Cut 2 large rectangles of parchment paper that is double the size of the fish.
    Place 3 lemon slices on each piece of parchment and place the fish directly on top. Season with salt and pepper, and add the tomatoes, tarragon and capers.

Fold the parchment paper around the edges tightly. Be sure to you press as you fold to seal the packets well, otherwise the steam will escape. Arrange the packets on a baking sheet. Bake until the fish is cooked through, about 12 minutes. Remove from oven and serve immediately.

Classic American Tuna Casserole

Tuna casserole is as easy to make as it is delicious! This heart-warming recipe is flexible, so you can replace the broccoli with your favorite veggie or the tuna with crab, lobster or salmon with equally fabulous results!

Ingredients

• Serves 4-6 •

2 (6-ounce) tins chunk light tuna packed in olive oil

1 tablespoon butter or olive oil

½ cup diced Spanish onion

½ cup diced celery

1 (8-ounce) can cream of mushroom soup

½ cup low-sodium vegetable broth

4 ounces chopped broccoli, blanched

1 cup buttered bread crumbs or crushed plain potato chips

8 ounces packaged wide noodles, cooked al dente

Directions

Preheat oven to 400°F.

Spray a glass casserole dish with vegetable oil. In a large saucepan, sauté onion and celery in the butter or olive oil until vegetables are barely soft. Add mushroom soup and vegetable broth. Bring to a simmer, stirring to dissolve soup. When it begins to boil, turn off heat and gently fold in the tuna and its oil. Add cooked pasta noodles, and toss to coat with sauce. Pour into prepared casserole and top with bread crumbs or potato chips. Bake 30-40 minutes until heated through and topping is lightly browned.

Black Bean & Wild Salmon Chili

Black beans have an earthy flavor that works well with seafood. My protein-packed recipe may sound like an unusual combination, but the creamy texture of black beans combined with the richness of wild salmon make them the perfect pair!

Ingredients

• Serves 6-8 •

1 pound dried black beans

1 bell pepper, chopped

1 medium onion, chopped

2 cloves garlic, chopped

3 cups low-sodium vegetable stock

4-6 cups water

1 tablespoon each dried cilantro, cumin, chili powder, cayenne and white pepper

¼ cup fresh cilantro, chopped

½ pound wild salmon, such as sockeye, Coho or Chinook, cut into chunks

Sea salt to taste

Vegetable oil for sautéing

• Optional toppings •

Sour cream, green onion, cheddar cheese,

tomatoes, avocado, mango, etc.

For the black beans

Soak black beans overnight. If you don't have time for soaking, cover the beans generously with cold water in a large saucepan and bring to a boil. Simmer for 2 minutes; remove from the heat, cover tightly with a lid and let them sit for 1 hour before using. Rinse beans until water runs clear. Set aside.

In a large soup pot, heat oil over medium heat. Add onions, bell peppers and garlic and sauté until soft, about 10 minutes. Mix in spices and stir for 2 minutes. Add the beans, water and vegetable stock to the pot and boil for 10 minutes. Add the sea salt, turn the heat to medium and allow the beans to simmer for 1 hour. After 1 hour, taste the beans for flavor and doneness. Adjust seasonings and cooking time as needed. The beans should be flavorful with a creamy texture.

For the wild salmon

Season salmon chunks with sea salt. Sauté for 4-6 minutes or until cooked through. Assemble the dish by adding a hearty scoop of black beans to a bowl, topped off with a few cubes of salmon. Add optional ingredients as desired. I enjoy mine with tomatoes, green onion and a little sour cream.

White Beans & Clams

Beans are an excellent source of fiber, folate and iron. Plus, they taste great! When I make white beans, I typically make a large batch from which I create several hearty dishes, including this White Beans and Clams recipe. If live clams are not available, you can replace them with shucked clams.

Ingredients

• Serves 6-8 •

4 pounds small live clams, such as littlenecks, well
rinsed and sorted for broken shells and debris

2 cups dried white beans

1 small Spanish onion, finely chopped

1 medium green bell pepper, finely chopped

2 tablespoons olive oil

3 cups low-sodium vegetable broth

1 cup clam juice

¼ cup coarsely chopped flat-leaf parsley

1 tablespoon fresh thyme, chopped finely

Sea salt to taste

Fresh cracked black pepper

Soak the beans overnight (or at least 8 hours) in 6-8 cups of cold water. If you don't have time for soaking, cover the beans generously with cold water in a large saucepan and bring to a boil. Simmer for 2 minutes, then remove from heat, cover tightly with a lid and let them sit for 1 hour. When ready to use, drain and rinse the beans. Transfer them to a large soup pot along with the 5 cups of water, vegetable broth, thyme, onion and green bell pepper. Bring to a boil for 10 minutes, then cover the pot and reduce the heat to medium. Simmer for 1 hour.

Next, add the clam juice and more water if necessary, as the beans should be covered completely.

Taste the beans for flavor and doneness. Adjust seasonings and cooking time as needed. The beans should be flavorful with a creamy texture. When the beans are done, add the clams and cover the pan tightly. Cook over moderate heat until the clams have opened—about 8 minutes. Spoon the beans and clams into bowls, garnish with the parsley and serve.

Seafood Jambalaya

Jambalaya is a Louisiana Créole dish of Spanish and French influence. My spicy version is chock-full of Gulf shrimp and my homemade smoked seafood sausage. You can add almost any seafood to this recipe with spectacular results.

Making the perfect jambalaya can be a bit tricky. Connoisseurs of the dish will tell you that the secret to a good bowl of jambalaya is perfectly cooked rice. So, be sure to keep an eye on your liquid levels and cooking time to ensure perfection!

Ingredients

· Serves 6-8 ·

½ pound smoked seafood sausage, sliced

1 pound U.S. Gulf shrimp, peeled, deveined, tails on

1 cup water

1 cup vegetable broth

½ cup bell pepper, chopped

½ cup celery, chopped

¼ cup onion, chopped

3 garlic cloves, minced

1 bay leaf

½ cup whole peeled canned tomatoes, chopped with juice

1 cup long-grain white rice

3 tablespoons vegetable oil

½ tablespoon each red pepper flakes, cayenne, paprika, white and black pepper

1 tablespoon herbes de Provençe

Salt to taste

· Optional toppings ·

Parsley or cilantro for garnish

Directions

Preheat oven to 375°F. In a deep cast-iron skillet or Dutch oven, sweat the bell pepper, garlic, celery, onion and tomatoes for about 4 minutes. (Sweating involves cooking food, typically vegetables, until they soften and cook in their own juices without browning.) Add herbs and spices and stir to combine. Turn the heat to medium high and add the seafood sausage and shrimp. Sauté for an additional 3 minutes. Add the rice and broth; stir to combine. The liquid should cover the ingredients; if not, add more water or broth. Cover the skillet and cook on the stove top for 10-12 minutes.

Place the dish in the oven for about 25 minutes, allowing the rice time to absorb the liquid. Taste the dish for doneness. The rice should be fully cooked and flavorful. If the rice is not cooked and a bit on the dry side, add warm water and cook for another 10 minutes. Remove from the oven when done and allow the dish to rest for 5 minutes before serving. Garnish with parsley or cilantro.

Grilled Lobster with Lemon-Infused Ghee

Right around Valentine's Day, my inbox is flooded with emails requesting lobster recipes. My best advice is to prepare this pricy crustacean as simply as possible—allowing the full, decadent flavor to shine through. I prefer to grill or broil whole lobsters and serve them with lemon-infused ghee.

Ingredients

· Serves 2 ·

2 whole Maine lobsters

1 cup ghee (traditional Indian clarified butter used for cooking)

2 tablespoons fresh tarragon, minced

1 lemon, juice and zest

Rustic Italian bread

Directions

Start by adding the ghee to a small sauce pan on low heat. Add the lemon zest and steep for
5 minutes. Remove from the heat and set aside.

Prepare the lobster

Drop 1 lobster, head first, into large pot of boiling water. Cover; cook 3 minutes (lobster will not be
fully cooked). Using tongs, transfer lobster to baking sheet. Return water to boil. Repeat with
second lobster.

Transfer 1 lobster, to work surface. Place tip of large knife into center of lobster. Cut lobster lengthwise in
half from center to end of head (knife may not cut through shell), then cut in half from center to end of
tail. Use poultry shears to cut through shell. Repeat with second lobster.

Prepare the grill on medium-high heat

Keeping lobster halves meat side up, brush shells with ghee. Place halves, meat side up, on the grill. Brush
meat with more lemon-infused ghee and sprinkle with tarragon.

Close the grill and allow the lobsters to cook until just opaque in thickest portion of tail, 7–9 minutes.
Drizzle a bit of lemon juice over the lobster and serve with the lemon-infused ghee and rustic
Italian bread.

Pineapple Blaff

Blaff is a traditional way of preparing fish throughout the
Caribbean, especially on the island of Martinique. The technique
is a combination of marinating and poaching.

Ingredients

• Serves 4 •

2 pounds white fish fillets or steaks

4 cups water

¼ cup lime juice

4 scallions, chopped (white and green)

½ cup pineapple juice

1 Scotch bonnet or other hot chili pepper, minced

3 garlic cloves, minced

½ cup minced onion

2 bay leaves

2 allspice berries

4 bunches parsley

1 tablespoon thyme

Freshly ground black peppercorns

1 teaspoon sea salt

Lime wedges for serving

Rinse the fish in cold water and cut each in half lengthwise. Next, add the fish along with 2 cups of the water and all the remaining ingredients (except the lime wedges) to a large, nonreactive bowl.

Cover and let the fish marinate in the refrigerator overnight. Remove the fish from the marinade and set aside. Add the marinade and the remaining 2 cups of water to a large pot and bring to a boil over medium-high heat. Reduce heat to medium low and simmer for about 5 minutes.

Add the fish to the simmering broth and simmer for another 10 minutes, or until the fish is cooked through and flakes easily. Serve with lime wedges.

Salmon and Mango Quesadilla

A quesadilla is essentially flour or corn tortillas stuffed with a mixture of cheese and other ingredients, then folded in half to form a half-moon shape. It can be sweet or savory. My quesadilla is a bit of both, thanks to succulent salmon and ripe mango slices. This recipe works equally as well with crab.

Ingredients

• Serves 4 •

4 (8-inch) flour tortillas

1 cup cooked salmon

½ cup cooked black beans

2 cups shredded Mexican cheese blend (Monterey Jack, cheddar)

¼ cup Cotija cheese

¼ cup chevre (goat cheese)

1 ripe mango, sliced thin

Cooking spray or vegetable oil for grilling

• Optional toppings •

Avocado slices, sour cream, tomato, cilantro or salsa.

Heat a large grill pan on medium high heat. Place 1 tortilla in the skillet. Flip it a couple of times with a spatula and remove it from the heat. Do this for each tortilla to help them warm up before stuffing.

Stuffing the tortillas

With the tortilla lying flat, add enough of the Mexican cheese blend to cover half of the tortilla. Next sprinkle on the Cotija cheese, chevre, black beans and salmon. Artfully add the slices of mango and fold over to make a half-moon shape. Do this for each tortilla.

Cooking the quesadillas

Over medium heat, add cooking spray or vegetable oil to the large grill pan and add 1 quesadilla. Adjust the heat to low and cook for 3 minutes on each side, allowing the cheese to melt. When the cheese has melted and the outside of the tortilla is crispy, remove from the heat. Cook the others.

Serve immediately with your choice of avocado slices, sour cream, tomato, cilantro or salsa.

Jerk Shrimp

My fascination with the Caribbean began at the age of 10 when my dad introduced me to the music of Bob Marley. I found the food and the culture of the island to be as infectious as the music. My interest deepened when I discovered that my maternal great-great-grandpa was from Barbados. I have been exploring the entire region with fervor ever since!

Research highlights the fact that jerk seasoning, in all its variations, was originally used as a method for preserving food. It has now grown into a cottage industry—there are literally thousands of prepared jerk marinades and spice blends on the market. My recipe is fabulous, and I encourage you use my version as a road map to creating your own unique blend.

Ingredients

• Serves 4-6 •

2 pounds of U.S. Gulf shrimp, cleaned and deveined

1 tablespoon each Jamaican allspice, whole cloves, whole black peppercorns, dried thyme and sea salt

6 green cardamom pods

½ inch fresh ginger root (cut into pieces)

2 garlic cloves

½ habañero pepper

1 scallion, chopped (green and white part)

2 limes (zest and juice)

2 tablespoons of olive oil

With a mortar and pestle, pound all of the dried spices individually until ground and fragrant. You will need to remove the hull from the cardamom pods. Do this by pounding them lightly until the husk falls off, revealing the black seeds. Throw out the husks and pound the black seeds until ground and fragrant. Place spices in a medium-sized bowl.

Next, pound the garlic, ginger, habañero pepper and green onion in the mortar and pestle until the mix forms a chunky consistency. Add these ingredients to the spice bowl along with the lime zest, lime juice and olive oil. Mix the ingredients to combine. Add the shrimp and marinate for 30 minutes. Grill for 3 minutes on each side, until the shrimp is pink and firm.

Fried Oysters

Some people dream of starting a tomato garden, I dream of starting an oyster farm! I simply can't get enough of these briny bivalves. And I get it honestly; my dad is a serious oyster hound!

My fried oysters can be stuffed into a sandwich, served atop a salad or eaten moments from leaving the frying pan. I prefer to use jars of oysters for this recipe—save the fresh-shucked oysters for roasting or enjoying on the half shell.

Ingredients

· Serves 2 ·

2 (8-ounce) jars oysters, drained

1 tablespoon cayenne pepper

2 teaspoons sea salt

1 teaspoon white pepper

1 teaspoon dried lavender, crushed

1 teaspoon dried thyme

2 cups corn flour

1½ cups canola oil for frying

Directions

In a medium-sized bowl, add the oysters along with the salt, cayenne pepper, dried lavender, white pepper and thyme. Mix to combine. Allow to marinate for 15 minutes. Add 1 cup of vegetable oil to a deep skillet and heat to 375°F.

In a separate bowl, add the corn flour and half the oysters. Gently toss the oysters in the corn flour to coat. Set the oysters aside and allow them to rest for 5 minutes–this will allow them to form a crust. Proceed with the other oysters. Fry the oysters 3 minutes per side until golden brown. Serve in a sandwich, atop a bed of greens or simply enjoy as is.

Mahi Mahi Tacos with Chipotle Sauce

Mahi-mahi means "strong-strong" in Polynesian. My version of mahi-mahi tacos yields strong and delicious flavor. Try this same recipe with shrimp, halibut, pollock or rock fish.

Ingredients

• Serves 6-8 •

1 pound mahi-mahi fillet, diced

1 lime, zest and juice

¼ cup cilantro, chopped

¼ cup white onion, thinly sliced

6 ounces cooked black beans, rinsed

½ cup strained Greek yogurt

2 chipotle peppers, seeded and minced

2 tablespoons toasted cumin

1 teaspoon garlic, granulated

Sea salt

Pepper, freshly cracked

2 tablespoons olive oil

12 corn or flour tortillas

Mexican blend cheese

Hass avocado slices

Red cabbage, sliced thinly

Directions

Mix the yogurt and chipotle chili and chill in the refrigerator. In a bowl, mix the mahi-mahi, lime zest, lime juice, cilantro, onion, garlic, sea salt, pepper, cumin and olive oil and marinate for 30 minutes. Add 2 tablespoons of olive oil to a grill pan and add the mahi-mahi. Sauté for 4 minutes, turning the fish intermittently. Cover and remove from heat. Warm the black beans and grill the tortillas according to package directions. To assemble the tacos, fill each tortilla with pieces of mahi-mahi, cheese, avocado, black beans and cabbage topped with the chipotle sauce.

Herb Roasted Oysters

I simply can't eat enough of these delicious delicacies. One dozen oysters can either be split as an appetizer between two people or as a main meal for one.

Ingredients

• Makes a dozen oysters •

½ cup panko bread crumbs

2 tablespoons ghee

1 tablespoon mixed fresh herbs (thyme, tarragon, basil)

1 teaspoon sea salt

1 dozen fresh oysters on the half shell

1 tablespoon parmesan cheese, grated

1 pound of kosher salt for bottom of baking sheet to help secure oysters

Directions

Preheat the oven broiler

Start by blending the panko bread crumbs with the ghee, herbs and sea salt. Add the kosher salt to the baking sheet and add the oysters, making sure that each is secure. Next, top each oyster with the bread crumb mixture and sprinkle on the parmesan cheese. Broil for 5 minutes. Serve immediately.

How to Shuck an Oyster

1. Generally, an oyster will have a flat side and a round side. With the flat side up, hold the oyster very steady on the table with the palm of your hand.
2. Where the oyster comes to a point (at its anterior edge), you will find the hinge where the two half shells are connected. The first step in shucking an oyster is to break the hinge.
3. Take an oyster knife and carefully force the tip of the knife into the hinge. It may take a little practice to find the right angle for each individual oyster, so just be patient (try to aim the knife at the table and not at your hand).
4. Once you have the tip of the knife inside the hinge, you will have to pry the two half shells apart. This may take twisting or turning the knife—find the angle that gives you're the most leverage.
5. Once the hinge has been broken, drag the knife along the underside of the flat side, aiming for the adductor muscle, which is found on the right side of the oyster when the hinge is facing you. This muscle must be severed in order to remove the flat shell from the rest of the oyster.
6. Once you have removed the flat side, the last step is to sever the adductor muscle from the round side of the shell.

Spicy Atlantic Mackerel with Whole Wheat Spaghetti & Arugula

A member of the tuna family, mackerel is a delicious fish. Its firm, high-fat flesh is known for its bold, savory flavor. The best part is that mackerel is inexpensive and can be found in most markets. My spicy whole wheat pasta recipe is ideal for anyone looking to create a simple, elegant, budget-friendly meal in minutes. Tinned skinless sardines in olive oil work equally as well for this recipe.

Ingredients

• Serves 4-6 •

6 ounces tinned mackerel in olive oil

1 pound whole wheat spaghetti

3 roma tomatoes, diced

1 cup wild arugula, rinsed and chopped

1 tablespoon fresh thyme, chopped

1 teaspoon red pepper flakes

2 tablespoons fresh lemon juice

3 tablespoons olive oil

¼ cup freshly grated parmesan cheese

2 teaspoons sea salt

1 teaspoon freshly cracked black pepper

Directions

Start by adding the mackerel and its oil in a small bowl. Flake the mackerel, add the diced tomatoes and set aside. Next cook the pasta to al dente according to package directions, drain and add to the large bowl. Add the olive oil, lemon juice, salt, thyme, pepper, red pepper flakes and arugula. Toss and taste. Adjust seasoning as required. Finally, toss in the freshly grated parmesan cheese. Serve immediately.

Wasabi Crusted Sea Scallops

These crispy wasabi-crusted sea scallops can be used as an appetizer or as a main dish. Be sure to use dry sea scallops for this recipe. Dry sea scallops are firmer in texture and have a better taste and texture better than "wet" scallops that have been treated with a preservative that can make them soft and milky.

Ingredients

• Serves 4-5 •

1½ pounds dry sea scallops, rinsed and dried

2 cups panko bread crumbs

¼ cup wasabi powder

2 eggs

1 tablespoon water

3 tablespoons sesame oil

Soy sauce for dipping

Vegetable oil for pan frying, about 1 cup

Directions

Place the scallops in a single layer on a clean surface and sprinkle with the wasabi powder on both sides. Allow them to rest for 5 minutes. In the meantime, make an egg wash by combing the 2 eggs with 1 tablespoon of water and mix to combine.

Next crust the sea scallops by taking one and dipping it in the egg wash, then rolling it in the panko bread crumbs. Be sure to get an even coating on all sides. When all sea scallops are coated, set them aside for 5 minutes.

Add the oil to a skillet and heat to 375°F. When the oil reaches that temperature, gently fry each scallop for 2 minutes on each side until crispy—be careful not to disturb the breading when turning. Drain on paper towels. Serve with a side of soy sauce for dipping.

Purple Eggplant in Anchovy Tomato Sauce

I created this recipe after receiving a gift of beautiful purple eggplant from my sister Leslie. She and her hubby have a beautiful organic garden of my dad's design—he's a bit of a garden geek. I used flat anchovies in olive oil for this recipe, but anchovy paste works just as well.

Ingredients

· Serves 3 ·

1 large eggplant (aubergine)

Sea salt

4 flat anchovies preserved in olive oil

16 ounces tinned tomatoes, peeled

½ cup Spanish onion, diced

3 garlic cloves

2 teaspoons crushed red pepper flakes

½ cup olive oil, divided use

1 tablespoon fresh thyme

Pecorino Romano cheese, grated

Freshly cracked black pepper

Start by prepping the eggplant. Slice the eggplant in ¼-inch pieces length wise and lay on a baking sheet. Sprinkle sea salt over each piece—this will help bring out the moisture so that they grill crispy without absorbing too much oil. While the eggplant is prepping, start the anchovy tomato sauce by adding the tomatoes and garlic to a food processor and blending to a chunky consistency. In a medium-sized sauce pan, add 3 tablespoons of olive oil, Spanish onion and thyme. Sweat the onion for 5 minutes until transparent. Add the anchovies and cook for another 5 minutes until the anchovies dissolve. Pour in the tomato mixture and simmer for 30 minutes. The mixture will reduce and become thick and luscious.

Cook the eggplant

Blot the eggplant with paper towels to remove the excess moisture. Using a pastry brush, coat each side of the eggplant with olive oil. Heat a grill pan to high and add 2 tablespoons of olive oil. Add the eggplant and grill until the edges turn crispy.

Assemble the dish by placing one slice of eggplant on a plate and spooning some of the anchovy tomato sauce over. Add another slice of eggplant on top of the sauce and spoon on and more sauce. Sprinkle with Pecorino Romano cheese and serve immediately.

Note: If you have any leftover eggplant, I recommend dicing it and adding it to the sauce.

Clam & Mussel Pasta
with Cilantro Pesto

Creating this recipe was a lot of fun because I focused on using ingredients that I had available in my kitchen cupboard and refrigerator. I used tins of clams and mussels, and they work really well for this dish.

Ingredients

· Serves 4-6 ·

6-ounce tin of mussels, reserve the liquid for other use

6-ounce tin of clams, reserve the liquid for other use

1 pound whole wheat pasta

1½ cups cilantro, leaves and stems

2 garlic cloves

1½ cups avocado oil

3 tablespoons water

½ cup walnuts, toasted

¼ cup Pecorino Romano cheese, grated

1 tablespoon red pepper flakes

Fresh cracked black pepper to taste

Flat-leaf parsley for garnish

Directions

Start by making the pesto. Add the cilantro, garlic, Pecorino Romano cheese, toasted walnuts and water to a blender. Turn the blender on medium and slowly drizzle in the avocado oil to create a thick sauce. Next cook the pasta to al dente according to package directions. Drain and add to the large bowl. Add the clams, mussels, red pepper flakes and fresh cracked black pepper to the hot pasta—the residual heat will warm the shellfish through. Add the cilantro pesto to the pasta, clams and mussels and mix well. Serve hot with flat-leaf parsley to garnish.

Blackened Tilapia

Blackening seasoning is most often used with catfish or redfish, but my version works equally as well with tilapia. The firm texture of this sweet fish works well with the flavors from my spice blend. When tilapia isn't readily available, try this recipe with salmon, shrimp or whitefish.

Ingredients

• Serves 2-3 •

1 pound tilapia fillets, rinsed and dried

1 tablespoon each cayenne pepper, paprika, white pepper, sea salt, freshly ground black pepper

2 tablespoons fresh rosemary leaves

1 garlic clove, cut in half

1 tablespoon olive oil

Lemon wedges for garnish

Directions

Prepare the fish by rubbing the garlic over the flesh on both sides. Set aside. Preheat the oven to 400°F. Using a mortar and pestle, combine the sea salt and rosemary and pound to a fine powder. Add the cayenne, paprika, white pepper and black pepper and blend. Sprinkle the spice blend evenly over the fish on both sides, then pour on 1 tablespoon of the olive oil and rub the spicy mix into the fish. Allow the fish to marinate for 15 minutes.

Heat a large cast iron skillet to high heat. Add the fish to the pan and sear on one side for 4 minutes. Using a spatula, flip the fish and place it in the oven for 4 more minutes until done. Serve with lemon wedges.

Soups & Chowders

Regardless of the temperature outdoors, I love sitting down to a bowl (or two) of steaming hot soup. Chock-full of succulent seafood, fresh vegetables, herbs and spices, the recipes in this section include some of my favorite basic soups, most of which lend themselves to experimentation and ingredient substitutions. Explore the possibilities of each recipe by adding a bit more of this or a little less of that and make the recipe your own!

Sustainable Seafood Gumbo

Gumbo is a dish that represents the melting pot of cultures that exist along the greater Gulf Coast of the United States. I first learned to make this sumptuous dish from my aunt Joan. She taught me the secret to making a good roux, which is by far one of the most important steps in creating an incredible gumbo. Roux adds flavor, depth and body to the dish. My gumbo is lighter than most. If you want a more gravy-like consistency to your gumbo, consider increasing the amount of roux.

Ingredients

• Serves 6-8 •

½ cup all-purpose flour

½ cup plus 2 tablespoons vegetable oil

1 cup celery, chopped

1 cup bell pepper, chopped

1 cup Spanish onion, chopped

½ cup carrot, chopped

2 garlic cloves, chopped

3 cups vegetable broth

6 cups water

1 bay leaf

1 tablespoon fresh thyme

2 tablespoons herbes de Provençe

2 tablespoons ground shrimp

1 tablespoon freshly ground black pepper

1 tablespoon white pepper

1 tablespoon cayenne pepper

1 tablespoon paprika

2 Dungeness crabs, cleaned and broken into pieces

2 pounds Gulf shrimp, peeled and deveined, plus 2 shrimp, ground

1 pound hard-shelled clams, scrubbed

1 pound mussels, scrubbed

1 tablespoon gumbo filé

Sea salt

Directions

Start by adding the oil and flour to a large, heavy pot and cooking for 10 minutes, stirring continuously so that the flour does not burn. Stir in the celery, bell pepper, onion and carrot, and stir until vegetables have softened—about 10 minutes. Next add the vegetable broth, water and bay leaf. Stir to incorporate, bring to a boil and allow the liquid to cook for 15 minutes.

Add the thyme, garlic, herbes de Provençe, black pepper, white pepper, cayenne, paprika and ground shrimp to the pot. Stir to incorporate and bring the pot to a simmer. Cook for 10 minutes with the lid on.

Next add the crab, shrimp, mussels and clams. Boil on high with the lid on until the mussels and clams have opened, about 4 minutes. Add the gumbo filé and stir to incorporate. Taste the soup and make flavor adjustments as needed. Serve over cooked rice.

Spicy Clam Chowder

This recipe is one of my go-to favorites because I typically have all of the ingredients stocked and it's easy to prepare. Try using sweet potatoes for a change of pace.

Ingredients

· Serves 4-6 ·

2 tablespoon ghee (clarified butter) or olive oil

1 small Spanish onion, chopped finely

2 cloves garlic, chopped finely

2 tablespoons fresh thyme

2 (6-Ounce) cans clams and their juice

1 roasted red bell pepper, chopped

5 small russet potatoes, diced

3 cups water

Sea salt and pepper to taste

Directions

In a medium-sized soup pot, add the ghee, onions and garlic and sweat them for 10 minutes. Be careful not to brown them. Next add the thyme and sauté for 3-5 minutes, until the thyme become fragrant. Turn up the heat to medium and add roasted pepper and sauté for 2 minutes. Add the juice from 2 cans of clams, the water and potatoes. Bring to a boil and cook for 15 minutes or until the potatoes are tender. Taste for flavor. Finally, add the clams and season with salt and pepper to taste. Cook for 5 minutes and serve.

Fresh Clams in Miso Broth

The earthy, rich flavor of miso pairs well with succulent clams.

Ingredients

· Serves 2-4 ·

3 tablespoons freshly grated ginger

½ cup scallions, thinly sliced

3 tablespoons shiro miso paste (sweet white miso)

4 pounds live small hard-shell clams, scrubbed well

1 tablespoon white sugar

½ pound Japanese soba noodles

Directions

Simmer 2 cups of water in a large pot with the scallions and ginger for 6 minutes. Add the miso paste and sugar, whisking until smooth. Bring to a boil and add the clams. Cover the pot with a lid until the clams have steamed open—about 4 minutes. Turn off the heat and allow to rest. Cook the soba noodles in salted water per package instructions. Drain and rinse. To serve, divide the noodle among bowls and add the clams and broth.

Dungeness Crab Soup

Chunky and indulgent, this soup is a wonderful way to use Dungeness crab.

Ingredients

· Serves 2-4 ·

1½ pounds of crab meat, double checked for shells

1 cup Spanish onion, chopped

1 cup celery, chopped

1 tablespoon ghee (clarified butter)

1 tablespoon olive oil

1 bay leaf

1 teaspoon Dijon mustard

⅓ cup all-purpose flour

2½ cups bottled clam juice or seafood stock

2 teaspoons fresh thyme, minced

1½ cups coconut milk

⅓ cup sherry

1 teaspoon paprika

Sea salt and freshly ground black pepper to taste

Directions

In a large, heavy saucepan, cook the onion, celery, and bay leaf in the olive oil and ghee over moderate heat, continually stirring, until the vegetables are soft—about 12 minutes. Next stir in the flour and cook, continually stirring, for 2 minutes—make sure the flour does not brown. Add the clam juice (or seafood stock) and the fresh thyme and simmer for 5 minutes. Use a whisk to help keep the flour from lumping. Whisk in the cream, sherry and Dijon mustard and bring to a boil. Stir in the crabmeat and taste the soup before add the sea salt and black pepper. Bring to a boil for an additional 5 minutes before serving.

Mussels in Gingered Carrot Broth

Mussels are delicious and one of the most affordable shellfish varieties.
Their briny flavor and meaty texture pair well with my gingery carrot broth.

Ingredients

• Serves 2-3 •

2 garlic cloves, minced

2 tablespoons ghee (clarified butter)

1 cup fresh carrot juice

½ cup water

2 tablespoons fresh ginger, minced

3 pounds live mussels, scrubbed well and debearded

¼ cup chives, chopped

1 lime, juice and zest

Directions

In a large pot, cook the garlic in the ghee over medium heat for 1 minute—be careful not to burn it. Add the carrot juice, water and ginger, and bring to a boil until liquid reduces by half. Next add the chives, lime juice, lime zest and mussels. Cover pot with a lid and turn heat to high to steam until the mussels open. Shake the pot occasionally to encourage the mussels to open—this should take about 10 minutes. Discard any unopened mussels. Serve warm with whole wheat French bread or a side dish of your choice.

Creamy Coconut Salmon Chowder

Cold-weather comfort food at its best! My Asian-inspired salmon chowder with coconut milk is fabulous! I am lactose intolerant, so the coconut milk, instead of cow's milk or cream, makes this velvety chowder an enjoyable experience. You can make this your own by experimenting with adding curry powder, ras el hanout or any spice blend to change up the flavor.

Ingredients

· Serves 4-6 ·

2 cups cooked salmon, shredded

1½ cups coconut milk

2 cups water

1 cup low-sodium vegetable broth

1 medium Spanish onion, chopped

¼ cup carrot, diced

2 large russet potatoes, diced

1 cup celery, chopped

2 tablespoons ghee (clarified butter)

1 tablespoon olive oil

2 teaspoons white pepper

2 tablespoons all-purpose flour

1 tablespoon fresh thyme, minced

1 bay leaf

Sea salt and freshly crack black pepper to taste

Directions

In a large, heavy pot, add the ghee along with the Spanish onion, carrot and celery over medium heat. Sweat the vegetables for 5 minutes until the onion is transparent. Next stir in the flour and olive oil, continually stirring, for 2 minutes—make sure the flour does not brown.

Add the water, vegetable broth and coconut milk along with the thyme and bay leaf, and bring to a boil. Pour in the potatoes and turn down the heat to simmer. Simmer uncovered for 25 minutes. Add the cooked salmon and simmer for another 5 minutes. Taste for seasoning and add salt and pepper as desired. Serve warm.

Shrimp Pho'

I would eat pho', also known as Vietnamese noodle soup, every day if possible. The complex flavors found within the broth always keep my guests curious about the next bit. Keep in mind that my version of this soup is much simpler than the traditional version, but I think it works just as well. You be the judge!

Ingredients

• Serves 2-3 •

• Broth •

1 large onion, peeled and halved

2-inch piece fresh ginger root, peeled and halved lengthwise

3-inch cinnamon stick

1 star anise

2 cloves

1 teaspoon coriander seeds

4 cups unsalted seafood stock

2 teaspoons soy sauce

4 carrots, peeled and coarsely chopped

• Noodles •

½ pound dried flat rice noodles (known as bánh pho'; use ¹⁄₁₆-inch, ⅛-inch, or ¼-inch width depending on availability and preference)

• Toppings •

½ pound cooked U.S. shrimp (or tofu, crab, your choice)

Vegetables such as bok choy, napa cabbage, or broccoli

• Garnishes •

½ onion, very thinly sliced

2 scallions, thinly sliced

1 chili pepper (Thai bird, serrano, or jalapeño), sliced

1 lime, cut into wedges

½ cup bean sprouts

A large handful of herbs: cilantro, Thai basil, cilantro/saw-leaf herb

Hoisin sauce, sriracha (optional)

Directions

For the broth

Char onion and ginger over an open flame (holding with tongs) or directly under a broiler until slightly blackened, about 5 minutes on each side. Rinse with water.

In a large pot, dry-roast cinnamon, star anise, cloves, and coriander over medium-low heat, stirring constantly to prevent burning. When spices are aromatic, add seafood stock, soy sauce, carrots, and charred onion and ginger. Bring broth to a boil, reduce heat, and simmer, covered, for 30 minutes. Strain and keep hot until ready to serve.

For the noodles

While the broth is simmering, place noodles in a large bowl and cover with hot water. Let stand for 20-30 minutes or until tender but still chewy. Drain. (If soaking does not soften the noodles enough, blanch them in a pot of boiling water for a few seconds.)

For the toppings

While broth is simmering, prepare toppings as desired—cook the shrimp, slice and cook tofu, lightly steam or blanch vegetables, etc. Toppings should be unseasoned or only lightly seasoned so as not to interfere with the flavor of the broth.

To serve

Divide noodles between 2 bowls. Arrange toppings over noodles. Ladle about 2 cups of broth into each bowl. Serve with garnishes on the side, which diners should add to taste. Enjoy!

Sides & Extras

As a pescatarian, I enjoy an abundance of legumes, vegetables, fruit, whole grains and the occasional piece of chocolate. The recipes found in this section include some of my everyday favorites and may be used as side dishes or combined to make a complete meal.

Lemony Chive Potatoes

These potatoes are delicious served warm or cold.
They pair well with grilled, baked or broiled seafood.

Ingredients

• Serves 2-4 •

1 pound potatoes, such as fingerling, red or any waxy variety, sliced

Juice of ½ a lemon, about 3 tablespoons

3 tablespoons chopped fresh chives

4 tablespoons olive oil

Sea salt and ground pepper to taste

Directions

In a large pot of salted water, boil sliced potatoes until tender, about 12 minutes. Be careful not to overcook them or they will fall apart. When the potatoes are done, drain them and place them in a large bowl. Add enough olive oil to the potatoes to coat nicely, then squeeze on the lemon juice and sprinkle on the chives, salt and pepper. Taste and adjust seasoning as needed.

Hot-Water Corn Bread

As far as I know, one of the only uses for hot-water corn
bread is for eating with a steaming bowl of greens—mustard grams are my
favorite. My goal was to develop a version that could stand on its own.

Ingredients

• Serves 8-10 •

2 cups of fine corn meal

1 tablespoon garlic powder

1 tablespoon onion powder

½ teaspoon of dried thyme

1 teaspoon of sea salt

1 cup hot water

Oil for frying

Directions

In a large bowl add the corn meal, garlic powder, onion power, dried thyme and sea salt. Next add
the hot water ½ a cup at a time, mixing in between. The mix should be smooth and thick. Allow
the mix to rest for 5 minutes. Start by heating a skillet and oil to 350 degrees.

Using your hands, scoop out bits of mix and form small, flat patties—each should be about the size of
your palm. Fry them in the oil for 4 minutes on each side until golden brown. Drain on paper
towels. The hot-water corn bread should be crispy on the outside, firm and moist on the inside.

Grilled Asparagus

Super easy and delicious, these grilled asparagus spears go well with almost anything. Grilled over high heat, they remain crisp and flavorful.

Ingredients

· Serves 4-6 ·

2 pounds fresh green asparagus, trimmed and peeled

Olive oil

Sea salt and freshly ground black pepper

Directions

Start by adding 2 tablespoons of olive oil to a hot grill pan. Add the asparagus and season with sea salt and freshly ground black pepper. Sauté for 2-3 minutes, shaking the pan on occasion to ensure even cooking. Serve warm.

Avocado Salad

This luscious avocado salad couldn't be more simple or delicious.
I like to have this for a light lunch or serve it atop grilled or broiled fish.
To mix things up a bit, add cooked bay shrimp or bay scallops.

Ingredients

· Serves 2 ·

1 large, ripe Hass avocado, split in half and seed removed, diced

2 tablespoons lemon juice

2 teaspoons red onion, chopped

½ cup tomato, diced

Sea salt to taste

1 tablespoon olive oil

Directions

Add the chunks of avocado to a bowl along with the sea salt, tomato and red onion. Drizzle the lemon juice and olive oil over the ingredients and gently mix to combine. Make certain not to mash the avocado or guacamole will be the result. Serve immediately.

Sautéed Cabbage & Salmon Bacon

I know what you're thinking—salmon bacon? The process of making salmon bacon involves slowly baking sliced smoked salmon until it loses most of it moisture and becomes meaty and crumbly. You have to experience it for yourself.

Ingredients

• Serves 4 •

1 head of napa cabbage, rinsed and chopped

1 shallot, chopped

6 ounces smoked salmon, slices

1 garlic clove, minced

2 teaspoons olive oil

Salt and pepper to taste

Directions

To create the salmon bacon, place smoked salmon slices on a baking sheet and place in a preheated 375°F oven. Bake for 20 minutes, turning at the 10-minute mark. When done, remove from oven and allow to cool. Next, add olive oil to a hot pan along with the salmon bacon, Napa cabbage, garlic and shallot. Sauté for 4 minutes until the cabbage is cooked through yet crunchy. Serve immediately.

Betty's Medley

This is one of my mother's go-to vegetable recipes. You can use any type of squash and add just about any vegetable imaginable. For added flavor, throw in a bit of roasted corn.

Ingredients

• Serves 2-3 •

1 cup zucchini, sliced on the diagonal

1 medium Spanish onion, sliced thin

4 large roma tomatoes, peeled and diced

1 garlic clove, minced

1 tablespoon water

3 tablespoons olive oil

Sea salt and freshly ground black pepper

Directions

Add olive oil to a hot sauté pan and the add zucchini, onions and garlic. Cook on high heat for 2 minutes. Next, add the tomatoes, sea salt, water and freshly ground black pepper. Cook for another 2 minutes. Cover with a lid and turn off the stove. Allow the residual heat to cook the vegetables through. Serve immediately.

Ray's Organic Greens

Next to his family, my dad's most prized possession is his organic garden. Living in central California provides him with the ideal climate to grow almost everything—avocados, oranges, tomatoes, beans and greens of every kind.

Ingredients

· Serves 4 ·

4 bunches mustard greens, rinsed and chopped

2 tablespoons of adobo seasoning

2 garlic cloves

2 cups water

Directions

Add the 2 cups of water to a pot along with the adobo seasoning and the garlic cloves and bring to a boil. Next add the mustard greens. Turn the heat down to medium and simmer for 18 minutes or until the greens are tender. Serve warm.

Sesame Soba Noodles

Sesame oil adds a wonderful flavor and aroma to Japanese soba noodles. One of the best things about this recipe (aside from being delicious) is that it can be eaten hot or cold, which makes it perfect for a meal on the go.

Ingredients

• Serves 4 •

1 package (8 ounces) Japanese soba (buckwheat) noodles

2 tablespoons sesame oil

2 teaspoons sesame seeds

¼ cup cilantro

Thinly sliced green onions or chives for garnish

Directions

Cook soba noodles per package instructions. Drain and rinse with cold water, removing as much water from the noodles as possible. Add to a large bowl and toss with the sesame oil, sesame seeds and cilantro. Garnish with green onions and serve.

Twice-Cooked Brussels Sprouts

This has to be one of my favorite ways to cook Brussels sprouts—this method brings out their natural sweetness

Ingredients

· Serves 4 ·

2 pounds Brussels sprouts, rinsed

1 tablespoon sea salt

6 whole garlic cloves

1 teaspoon black pepper, freshly cracked

2 tablespoons olive oil

Directions

Heat your oven to 400°F. In a large steamer, steam the Brussels sprouts with the garlic for 10 minutes. Add the olive oil to a cast iron skillet and add the Brussels sprouts, garlic, black pepper and sea salt. Toss to coat evenly. Place the skillet in the oven and roast for 10 minutes. Serve immediately.

Fresh Tortilla Chips

This fresh tortilla chip recipe is so simple that it's hardly a recipe at all.
My niece, Courtney, requests that I make these chips (along with plenty of
fresh guacamole) every time she visits. I suspect that what makes them so
special is that I pan fry them in small batches.

Ingredients

· Serves 4 ·

24 corn tortillas, cut into triangles

3 cups canola oil, plus more as needed

Sea salt

Directions

In a deep skillet, heat 2 cups of canola oil to 375°F. Add the tortilla chips in small batches. Fry on each
side for 2 minutes, turning intermittently. Drain the chips on paper towels and sprinkle with sea salt.
Serve immediately. Start a new batch and add more oil to the skillet as required.

Spicy Yucatan Fruit Salad

Inspired by the fruit sold by street vendors in Mexico, my
spicy fruit is the perfect ending to any meal.

Ingredients

· Serves 4-6 ·

1 cup cantaloupe, diced

1 cup honeydew melon, diced

1 cup mango, seeded and diced

1 cup pineapple, peeled, cored and diced

1 cup papaya, seeded and diced

2 teaspoons ancho chili powder

1 lime, zest and juice

2 teaspoons sea salt

Directions

Add the cantaloupe, honeydew, pineapple, papaya and mango to a large bowl and toss with the
ancho chili powder, lime zest, lime juice and sea salt. Toss to coat and serve immediately.

Garlicky Spinach

This yummy spinach recipe works best with fresh spinach,
but it also works with the frozen variety in a pinch.

Ingredients

• Serves 2 •

2 pounds baby spinach, rinsed

4 cloves garlic, peeled and chopped

1 teaspoon red pepper flakes

3 tablespoons olive oil

1 teaspoon sea salt

Directions

In a large sauté pan, add the olive oil, garlic and red pepper flakes and cook over medium heat for
30 seconds. Add the spinach and sea salt, and sauté for 2 minutes. Serve immediately.

Steamed Corn on the Cob

Corn on the cob steamed in it husks tastes incredible. Wrapping
the corn in the husks is a bit labor intensive, but well worth the effort.

Ingredients

· Serves 12 ·

12 fresh ears of corn, husks reserved and silk removed

Directions

Preheat your grill or barbeque to medium heat.

Prepare the husks

Select 24 of the best-looking corn husks along with a few extras. Rinse the husks, making sure to remove
any silk that may be lingering. Tear the extra corn husks into strips lengthwise—these will be used to
tie the corn packets together.

Prepare the corn

Wrap each piece of corn in 2 husks, using the strips to secure the packet together. Add them to a
medium-hot grill and cook for 12-18 minutes with the lid closed.

Everyday Mediterranean Salad

This is my everyday salad that I typically have for lunch or serve as a side dish. It can also be served as a main meal with a nice piece of grilled fish. It is inspired by Mediterranean flavors, but you can add almost anything to this mix and it will taste great.

Ingredients

• Serves 2 •

3 cups romaine lettuce, rinsed and chopped

½ cup kidney beans

½ cup garbanzo beans (chickpeas)

½ cup tomatoes, chopped

½ cup marinated artichokes

3 ounces feta cheese, crumbled

Freshly cracked black pepper, to taste

6 pitted Kalamata olives

2 toasted pitas

• Vinaigrette •

¼ cup lemon juice

1 cup olive oil

1 tablespoon shallot, minced

Directions

Prepare the salad by adding equal portions of lettuce, kidney beans, garbanzo beans (chickpeas), tomato and marinated artichokes to each bowl. Top with crumbled feta and Kalamata olives.

For the vinaigrette, combine the lemon juice, black pepper and shallot in a bowl. Whisk the mixture and slowly drizzle in the olive oil in while whisking. Pour the vinaigrette over each salad. Serve with the toasted pita on the side or crumbled into the salad.

Sauces & Spice Blends

The recipes found throughout this section are
designed to take your taste buds on a culinary adventure!
By experimenting with the right blend of herbs and spices,
the most humble piece of fish can be transformed into an
exotic treat.

Harissa

Widely used in the African countries of Algeria, Morocco and Tunisia, harissa is a spicy chili-based sauce. It is often served as a side dish in which to dip vegetables, bread or grilled meat, or is stirred into stews and added to couscous.

Ingredients

• Makes ½ cup •

12 dried red chilies

1 tablespoon coriander seeds

2 teaspoons cumin seeds

2 garlic cloves

½ teaspoon sea salt

4-6 tablespoons olive oil

Directions

Discard the stems and some of the seeds from the chilies and soak them in warm water for 30 minutes until softened. Meanwhile, dry fry the coriander and cumin seeds to bring out the flavor and grind them to a powder. Pound the garlic with the salt, add the drained chilies and pound the mixture until it is smooth. Add the spices and gradually pound in the oil, trickling it in and mixing until the sauce is well blended and of a mayonnaise-like consistency.

Use the harissa at once or transfer it to an airtight jar. Add more olive oil to the top of the mix to make a seal. Cover and store in the fridge up to three weeks.

Ethiopian Berbere

This Ethiopian spice mix, pronounced "bari-baray," is a blend that is added to many dishes, including fish dishes and stews.

Ingredients

· Makes about ½ cup ·

10 dried red chilies

8 white cardamom pods

1 teaspoon cumin seeds

1 teaspoon coriander seeds

1 teaspoon fenugreek seeds

8 cloves

1 teaspoon allspice berries

2 teaspoons black peppercorns

1 teaspoon ajowan seeds

1 teaspoon ground ginger

½ teaspoon ground nutmeg

2 teaspoons sea salt

Directions

Discard the stalk end and some of the seeds from the chilies. Heat a heavy-based frying pan. Bruise the cardamom pods and add them to the pan with the cumin, coriander, fenugreek cloves, allspice, peppercorns and ajowan seeds. Toast the spices, shaking the pan over the medium heat, until they give off a rich aroma and just begin to turn color. Remove the seeds from the cardamom pods and then grind all the roasted spices to a fine powder. Mix in the ginger, nutmeg and salt. Use immediately or transfer to an airtight jar and store in the refrigerator up to 3 weeks.

Tsire Powder

This simple and delicious mix is used as a coating for grilled fish and meat throughout West Africa. Typically, raw fish is dipped in oil or beaten egg and then dipped in tsire powder. Additional tsire powder is sprinkled on the cooked fish when served.

Ingredients

• Makes ½ cup •

½ cup salted peanuts

¼ teaspoon cinnamon

¼ teaspoon cloves

¼ teaspoon ginger

¼ teaspoon nutmeg

¼ teaspoon allspice

½ teaspoon chili powder

Sea salt

Directions

Grind the peanuts to a coarse powder in a mortar, blender or food processor, then add the ground mixed spices, chili powder and a little salt. Use at once or transfer to an airtight container and store in the refrigerator for up to six weeks.

Kuala Lumpur Spicy Glaze

Inspired by the street food of Malaysia, this spicy
glaze can be used to top crispy fried fish.

Ingredients

• Makes about 1 cup •

12 small dried red chilies

3 tablespoons coriander seeds

1½ tablespoons fennel seeds

1 tablespoon cumin seeds

½ cup sugar

⅔ cup of molasses

½ cup fish sauce

½ cup low-sodium soy sauce

⅓ cup soy sauce

8 garlic cloves, peeled and mashed

2 tablespoons fresh ginger

Directions

In a skillet, toast the chilies and coriander, fennel and cumin seeds over medium heat until fragrant
(about 3 minutes). Transfer to a mortar and grind to a fine powder. Transfer to a medium bowl
and whisk in the sugar, molasses, fish sauce, soy sauces, ginger and garlic. Use immediately or
store in an airtight container in the refrigerator for up to 2 weeks.

Sticky Caribbean Mango Glaze

Part barbeque sauce, part glaze, this sauce works well with grilled shrimp, salmon, fried catfish nuggets and most white-fleshed fish.

Ingredients

• Makes about ½ cup •

½ large mango, peeled and cut into chunks

2 tablespoons sugar

1½ teaspoons tamarind paste

1 teaspoon Worcestershire sauce

½ teaspoon soy sauce

¼ teaspoon crushed red pepper

1 garlic clove, minced

1 tablespoon olive oil

1 teaspoon sea salt

Directions

In a blender, combine the mango with sugar, tamarind paste, Worcestershire sauce, soy sauce and crushed red pepper; puree until smooth. In a saucepan, heat the vegetable oil until shimmering, add the minced garlic and cook over medium heat until fragrant (about 1 minute). Add the mango puree, season with salt and bring the glaze to a simmer. Cook the glaze over low heat until thickened.

Rosemary Salt

I have an abundance of rosemary growing in my backyard. I really love the flavor of this savory fresh herb, but for my tastes it must be broken down into powder form in order to be palatable. The following recipe is one of my favorite ways to use rosemary.

Ingredients

· Makes about ½ cup ·

¼ cup sea salt

¼ cup fresh rosemary leaves

Directions

In stages, add the rosemary leaves and salt to a mortar and pestle; combine until blended into a crumbly, savory salt. Keeps for 2 to 3 weeks.

Perfect Papaya Salsa

I like the flavor of red Caribbean papaya for this recipe, but the strawberry variety will work just fine. Serve this alongside grilled fish, broiled fish or as a simple salad.

Ingredients

• Makes about 1½ cups •

1 cup red Caribbean papaya, chopped

¼ cup red onion, chopped

1 tablespoon fresh ginger, grated

¼ cup chopped cilantro

1 teaspoon ground cinnamon

1 tablespoon olive oil

Directions

Mix ingredients together and allow the salsa to rest for 5 minutes before serving.

My Favorite Jerk

This recipe is one of my favorite ways to bring the flavors of Jamaica to my kitchen. What I love most about jerk seasoning is how adaptable it is to a wide variety of spices. The one spice you can't forgo, however, is pimento, also known as allspice. My chunky version of jerk seasoning focuses on flavor instead of heat.

Ingredients

• Makes about ¼ cup •

1 tablespoon each Jamaican allspice, whole cloves,

whole black peppercorns, dried thyme and sea salt

6 green cardamom pods

½ inch fresh ginger root (cut into pieces)

2 garlic cloves

½ habañero pepper

1 scallion, chopped (green and white part)

2 limes (zest and juice)

2 tablespoons olive oil

Directions

With a mortar and pestle, pound all of the dried spices individually until ground and fragrant. You will need to remove the hull from the cardamom pods. Do this by pounding them lightly until the husk falls off, revealing the black seeds. Throw out the husks and pound the black seeds until ground and fragrant. Place spices in a small bowl.

Next, pound the garlic, ginger, habañero pepper and scallion with the mortar and pestle until the mix forms a chunky consistency. Add these ingredients to the spice bowl along with the lime zest, lime juice and olive oil. Mix the ingredients to combine. Use immediately or store in an airtight container in the refrigerator for up to 1 week.

Traditional Chimichurri Sauce

I was first introduced to the wonders of chimichurri sauce at an incredible Argentine restaurant on Melrose Avenue in Los Angeles. They served the sauce as a starter with fresh bread and atop fresh grilled wild salmon. I fell madly in love!

Ingredients

• Makes about 1 cup •

¼ cup coarsely chopped flat-leaf parsley

3 tablespoons red wine vinegar

4 large garlic cloves, very finely chopped

2 tablespoons oregano leaves, chopped

2 teaspoons crushed red pepper

Sea salt and freshly crushed black pepper

½ cup extra virgin olive oil

Directions

Mix ingredients together and allow the sauce to marinate for 15 minutes before using. Use immediately or store in an airtight container in the refrigerator for up to 2 weeks.

Moroccan Spice Rub

A yummy blend of savory and sweet, this rub works
well on salmon, black cod and vegetables.

Ingredients

· Makes about ⅓ cup ·

1 tablespoon ground coriander

1 tablespoon ground cumin

1 tablespoon ground chili powder

1 tablespoon light brown sugar

1½ teaspoons sea salt

1 teaspoon cinnamon

½ teaspoon caraway seeds, crushed

½ teaspoon freshly ground black pepper

Directions

In a small bowl, combine all of the ingredients—be sure to remove any lumps from the brown sugar. One of my favorite uses for this rub is on top of salmon before broiling. Use immediately or store in an airtight container in the refrigerator for up to 2 weeks.

Spicy Mexican Pesto

This version of pesto has a Mexican twist with the addition of cilantro and jalapeño pepper.

Ingredients

• Makes approximately 1 cup •

1 cup cilantro, leaves and stems

½ cup flat-leaf parsley, leaves and stems

1 garlic clove

1 tablespoon fresh ginger

1 tablespoon lemon juice

½ large jalapeno pepper, seeded and chopped

½ cup vegetable oil

Salt to taste

Directions

In a blender, mince the cilantro, parsley, garlic, ginger, lemon juice and jalapeño pepper. With the machine running, gradually add the oil in a steady stream and puree ingredients. Scrape the sides as needed. Add to a bowl and add salt to taste. Use immediately or store in an airtight container in the refrigerator for up to 1 week.

Turkish Baharat

This savory Turkish spice mix can be used to season fish, vegetables or rice.

Ingredients

• Makes 4 tablespoons •

1 tablespoon dried oregano

1 tablespoon pickling spice

1 teaspoon freshly ground black pepper

½ teaspoon cinnamon

½ teaspoon cumin

½ teaspoon dried mint

¼ teaspoon freshly grated nutmeg

½ teaspoon dried ground rosebuds

½ teaspoon ground cloves

Directions

In a small bowl, blend together all ingredients until combined well. Spice blend keeps in an airtight container at cool room temperature up to 2 months.

Mango Habeñero Sauce

This spicy recipe is my version of delicious sauce that comes from the Philippines. Try to find cebu or Filipino mangoes for this recipe.

Ingredients

• Makes about 1½ cup •

1 habañero pepper

5 cebu mangoes, chopped

1 habañero pepper

2-inch piece ginger, minced

½ cup freshly squeezed lime juice

¼ cup water

Directions

Roast the habañero over a flame or in a skillet set over medium heat until the skin blisters and blackens a bit and the chili softens. Remove from heat.

Add the mango, habañero, ginger, water and lime juice to a blender. Combine until smooth. Pour into a medium saucepan, cover, and set over medium-low heat. Allow to simmer for 10 minutes. Use immediately or store in an airtight container in the refrigerator for up to 1 week.

Ras el Hanout

Aromatic and luxurious, ras el hanout, or "head of the shop," is one of my favorite spice blends. Like most spice blends, there is no authoritative recipe. Ras el hanout is widely used in North Africa and can contain up to 20 different spices. Mine contains slightly less. Have fun with this recipe and experiment as you will.

Ingredients

· Makes about ¼ cup ·

1 teaspoon ground cumin

1 teaspoon ground ginger

1 teaspoon turmeric

1 teaspoon salt

1 teaspoon lavender

1 teaspoon dried flowers

¼ teaspoon ground cardamom seeds

¾ teaspoon ground cinnamon

¾ teaspoon freshly ground black pepper

½ teaspoon ground white pepper

½ teaspoon ground coriander seeds

½ teaspoon cayenne

½ teaspoon ground allspice

½ teaspoon ground nutmeg

¼ teaspoon ground cloves

Directions

In a small bowl blend together all ingredients until combined well. Spice blend keeps in an airtight container at cool room temperature 1 month.

Chunky Mango Avocado Salsa

The last time I brought this salsa to a party, there was a
fight over who would get the last scoop.

Ingredients

• Makes 2 cups •

1 large ripe mango, peeled, seeded and chopped into ¼-inch chunks

1 large ripe avocado, peeled, seeded and chopped into ¼-inch chunks

¼ cup red onion, chopped

¼ cup cilantro, chopped

1 teaspoon fresh garlic

1 tablespoon green onion, chopped

1 large lime (zest and juice)

Salt and pepper to taste

Direction

In a medium-sized glass bowl, add mango and all of the veggies, garlic and chopped cilantro. Mix well.
Add the zest and juice of the lime along with salt and pepper to taste. Cover with plastic wrap and
chill mix in the refrigerator for 15 minutes to allow flavors to blend. After 15 minutes add avocado
and gently mix.

Chunky Guacamole

In my home state of California, avocados are king! My delicious version of chunky guacamole is fantastic served with fresh tortilla chips, stuffed into tacos or served atop grilled fish. Hass avocados are perfect for this recipe because they are firm, buttery and full of flavor.

Ingredients

• Makes 1½ cups •

4 ripe Hass avocados, seeded and chopped into chunks

¼ cup finely chopped cilantro

¼ cup finely chopped red onion

1 teaspoon cayenne pepper

1 garlic clove, chopped finely

1 large lime, zest and juice

1 tablespoon sea salt

Direction

In a medium-sized bowl, combine all of the ingredients and mix until combined. Serve immediately.

Anchovy and Eggplant Sauce

Also known as aubergine, melongene, brinjal or guinea squash, eggplant is simply divine! I love its meaty, succulent texture. You will find a similar recipe in the main-course section of the book called Purple Eggplant in Anchovy Tomato Sauce. This version is assembled differently and used as a dip for crostini, served atop grilled fish or mixed with pasta.

Ingredients

· Makes 2 cups ·

1 large eggplant (aubergine)

Sea salt

16 ounces tinned tomatoes, peeled

3 garlic cloves

½ cup Spanish onion, diced

2 teaspoons crushed red pepper flakes

½ cup olive oil, separated

1 tablespoon fresh thyme

Freshly cracked black pepper

4 flat anchovies preserved in olive oil

Direction

Start by prepping the eggplant. Dice the eggplant in ¼-inch pieces and lay on a baking sheet. Sprinkle sea salt over each piece—this will help bring out the moisture so that they grill crispy without absorbing too much oil. While the eggplant is prepping, start the anchovy tomato sauce by adding the tomatoes and garlic to a food processor and blending to a chunky consistency. In a medium-sized sauce pan, add 3 tablespoons of olive oil, Spanish onion and thyme. Sweat the onion for 5 minutes until transparent. Add the anchovies and cook for another 5 minutes until the anchovies dissolve. Pour in the tomato mixture and simmer for 30 minutes. The mixture will reduce and become thick and luscious.

Cook the eggplant

Blot the eggplant with paper towels to remove the excess moisture. Coat the eggplant with olive oil. Heat a grill pan to high and add 2 tablespoons of olive oil. Add the eggplant and sauté until the edges turn crispy.

Assemble the sauce by adding the eggplant and adding it to the tomato sauce. Cook for another 10 minutes to allow the flavors to meld. Serve with crostini, atop grilled fish or mix with pasta.

Volume

1 US tablespoon • 3 US teaspoons
1 US fluid ounce • 29.57353 milliliters (ml)
1 US cup • 16 US tablespoons
1 US cup • 8 US fluid ounces
1 US pint • 2 US cups
1 US pint • 16 US fluid ounces
1 liter (l) • 33.8140227 US fluid ounces
1 liter (l) • 1000 milliliters (ml)
1 US quart • 2 US pints
1 US gallon • 4 US quarts
1 US gallon • 3.78541178 liters

Weight

1 milligram (mg) • 0.001 grams (g)
1 gram (g) • 0.001 kilograms (kg)
1 gram (g) • 0.035273962 ounces
1 ounce • 28.34952312 grams (g)
1 ounce • 0.0625 pounds
1 pound (lb) • 16 ounces
1 pound (lb) • 0.45359237 kilograms (kg)

1 kilogram (kg) • 1000 grams
1 kilogram (kg) • 35.273962 ounces
1 kilogram (kg) • 2.20462262 pounds (lb)
1 stone • 14 pounds
1 short ton • 2000 pounds
1 metric ton • 1000 kilograms (kg)

Length

1 centimeter (cm) • 10 millimeters (mm)
1 inch • 2.54 centimeters (cm)
1 foot • 0.3048 meters (m)
1 foot • 12 inches
1 yard • 3 feet
1 meter (m) • 100 centimeters (cm)
1 meter (m) • 3.280839895 feet
1 furlong • 660 feet
1 kilometer (km) • 1000 meters (m)
1 kilometer (km) • 0.62137119 miles
1 mile • 5280 ft
1 mile • 1.609344 kilometers (km)
1 nautical mile • 1.852 kilometers (km)

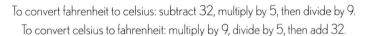

To convert fahrenheit to celsius: subtract 32, multiply by 5, then divide by 9.
To convert celsius to fahrenheit: multiply by 9, divide by 5, then add 32.

Fahrenheit (degrees F)	Celsius (degrees C)	Gas Number	Oven Terms
225 degrees F	110 degrees C	¼	Very Cool
250 degrees F	130 degrees C	½	Very Slow
275 degrees F	140 degrees C	1	Very Slow
300 degrees F	150 degrees C	2	Slow
325 degrees F	165 degrees C	3	Slow
350 degrees F	177 degrees C	4	Moderate
3/5 degrees F	190 degrees C	5	Moderate
400 degrees F	200 degrees C	6	Moderately Hot
425 degrees F	220 degrees C	7	Hot
450 degrees F	230 degrees C	8	Hot
475 degrees F	245 degrees C	9	Hot
500 degrees F	260 degrees C	10	Extremely Hot
550 degrees F	290 degrees C	10	Broiling

Sources

The following list of sources will help you make informed decisions about the seafood you choose and help you understand challenges facing our oceans.

FishWatch, http://www.nmfs.noaa.gov/fishwatch/
> FishWatch is sponsored by National Oceanic and Atmospheric Administration (NOAA) Fisheries Service, the U.S. authority on marine fisheries science, conservation and management. The goal of FishWatch is to help consumers make informed decisions about seafood by providing the most accurate and up-to-date information on seafood available in the United States. NOAA is a federal agency focused on the condition of the oceans and the atmosphere.

Monterey Bay Aquarium, http://www.montereybayaquarium.org/cr/seafoodwatch.aspx
> The Monterey Bay Aquarium's Seafood Watch program is focused on helping consumers and businesses make choices for healthy oceans. The program's recommendations indicate which seafood items are "Best Choices," "Good Alternatives," and those to "Avoid."

Environmental Protection Agency (EPA),
http://water.epa.gov/scitech/swguidance/fishshellfish/fishadvisories/advisories_index.cfm
> The EPA's mission is to protect human health and the environment. As such, the agency offers educational information about the benefits and challenges associated with eating seafood, advice for women of child-bearing age and children, and local fish advisories.

U.S. Food and Drug Administration (FDA),
http://www.fda.gov/food/foodsafety/Product-SpecificInformation/Seafood/default.htm
> The FDA operates a mandatory safety program for all fish and fishery products. The FDA program includes research, inspection, compliance, enforcement, outreach and the development of regulations and guidance. As a cornerstone of that program, FDA publishes the Fish and Fisheries Products Hazards and Controls Guidance, an extensive compilation of the most up-to-date science and policy on the hazards that affect fish and fishery products and effective controls to prevent their occurrence. This document has become the foundation of fish and fishery product regulatory programs around the world.

Centers for Disease Control and Prevention (CDC),
http://www.atsdr.cdc.gov/toxfaqs/tf.asp?id=113&tid=24
> The CDC's mission is to collaborate to create the expertise, information and tools that people and communities need to protect their health—through health promotion; prevention of disease, injury and disability; and preparedness for new health threats.

Gotmercury.org, http://www.gotmercury.org/article.php?list=type&type=75

Gotmercury.org is part of Turtle Island Restoration Network's efforts to protect the environment and the public from mercury. The network's Got Mercury? Calculator helps consumers make healthier seafood choices. Just enter your weight, the seafood type and the amount of seafood you will eat during a week, and click the calculator button. These calculations are based on EPA and FDA data.

Marine Stewardship Council (MSC), http://www.msc.org/

The MSC is the world's leading certification and ecolabelling program for sustainable seafood. Look for the blue MSC ecolabel when shopping or dining out. The MSC has developed standards for sustainable fishing and seafood traceability. Both standards meet the world's toughest best-practice guidelines and are helping to transform global seafood markets.

KidSafe Seafood Program, www.kidsafeseafood.org

The KidSafe Seafood Program helps to minimize the confusion about what species and which quantities of seafood are safe for children to consume. The program encourages greater scientific clarity and government fish consumption guidelines for kids, works to create demand for healthy and sustainable seafood and educates parents about which seafood is best for their children and for the ocean.

Fish 4 Your Health, http://fn.cfs.purdue.edu/fish4health/index.html

Fish 4 Your Health is intended to help pregnant or nursing women make informed decisions about the seafood that they consume. The program encourages pregnant or nursing women and women that will become pregnant to follow several recommendations that will help their babies to be healthy. Program cooperators include experts from Purdue University, Indiana Department of Environmental Management, Indiana Department of Health, Rhode Island Sea Grant, Washington Sea Grant, Illinois-Indiana Sea Grant, Texas Sea Grant, Florida Department of Health and the Aquarium of the Pacific (Long Beach).

Natural Resources Defense Council, http://www.nrdc.org/oceans/seafoodguide/

The Natural Resources Defense Council's purpose is to safeguard the Earth: its people, its plants and animals and the natural systems on which all life depends. The organization works to restore the integrity of the elements that sustain life—air, land and water—and to defend endangered natural places. The council offers a sustainable seafood guide and information about shopping for local seafood.

Au revoir

Thanks for buying my cookbook! I hope you had as much
fun using it as I did creating it. I encourage you to be fearless
in the kitchen and to experiment with the wide variety of
sustainable seafood options available. Until next time!

Stephanie, The Posh Pescatarian

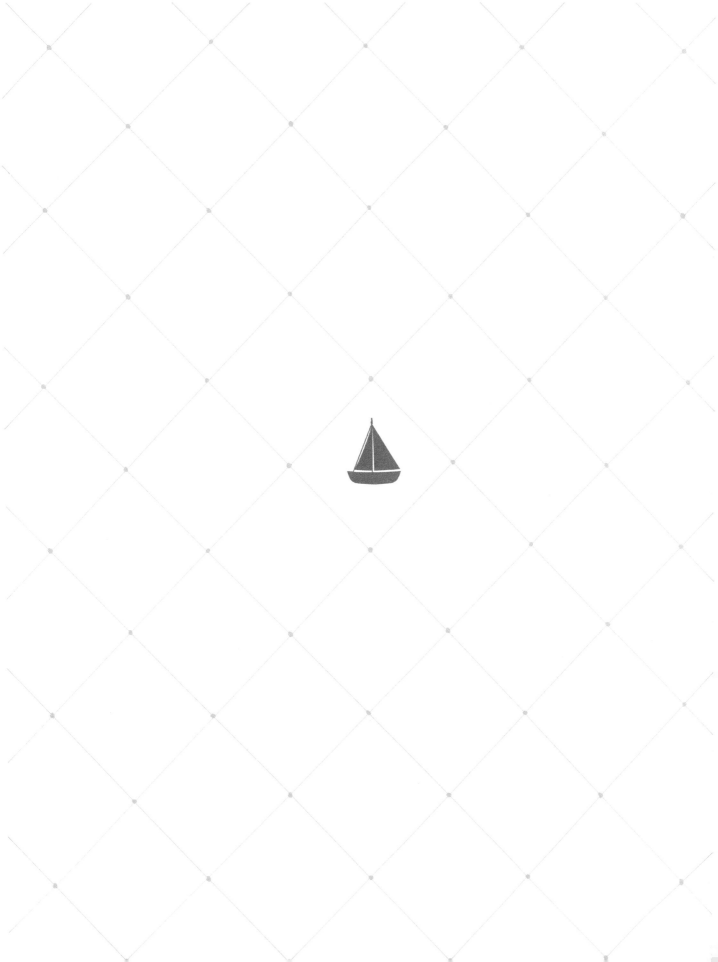

Made in the USA
Lexington, KY
24 July 2013